# TANTRIC
# Mothering

## A Path of Practical Love, Spiritual Growth & Planetary Change

## Didi Ananda Uttama

Neohumanist College of Asheville Press
North Carolina

Tantric Mothering: A Path of Practical Love, Spritual Growth, and Planetary Change
Copyright © 2024 by Didi Ananda Uttama

Published in the United States by
Neohumanist College of Asheville Press
160 Wellness Way Marshall, NC 28753
nhca.gurukul.edu
info@nhca.gurukul.edu

Library of Congress Control Number: 2024922800

ISBN: 978-1-957460-04-8

Cover and Layout: Iris Heddes

The Neohumanist College of Asheville was founded in 2015. In the words of Shri P.R. Sarkar, Neohumanism is "the (cultivation) of love for all created beings of the universe." The College's mission is to share knowledge that cultivates a Neohumanist vision and fosters creating sustainable futures for all.

# What readers are saying about
## Tantric Mothering

This is a wonderful book for the new mother who considers herself a spiritual being. Both inspiring and illuminating, it helps us understand that infants are engulfed in joy, and how we as mothers can "carry the child's mind along in the current of joy." I recommend this book to all mothers. Every mother wants to have a joyful attachment with her infant.

— *Vimala McClure*, *author, Infant Massage: a Handbook for Loving Parents and founder of the International Association of Infant Massage*

This book is an Ode to Love. It illustrates the unique bond that exists between mothers and their children, showing what this loving relationship could be at its best. Moreover, this loving bond is linked to Yogic/Tantric spiritual practices - taken together, they can lead to a higher level of self-realisation as well as progressive social change. Didi Ananda Uttama frames mother-child relationship as the ultimate example of coordinated cooperation and partnership model. It is from this relationship that we could all learn and evolve toward that very rare of permanent things in this world - the Infinite Love.

— *Ivana Milojevic*, *researcher and educator, Metafuture.org*

This book is a treasure trove just for you whether you are a first time parent or a third time parent. It runneth over with precious gems of which you may or may not be aware. Reading about the diverse experiences of so many parents-to-be and how they are navigating this journey of birth and welcoming a new family member is very heart-warming and enlightening. There is a shining light in here for every new parent. Please sample this delicious treat!

— *MJ Glassman*, *yoga preschool director and Neohumanist educator*

A wonderfully inspirational book. For all those who are caring for babies and young children, as well as interested others, this delightful book is about the links between joyous and transcendental devotional love and spirituality. It affected my relationship with my child in a very positive way, so that I trust her and listen to her more.

— *Marguerite Camilieri*, *lecturer at University of Malta*

As a mother of four daughters and grandmother of two boys, I have experienced first-hand what Didi has so successfully shared. She has captured the Essence of Motherhood. I am thrilled that Didi's book will empower women in their journey of Mother and Womanhood.

— *Laura Foti Liverakos*, *doula, LaLeche League leader, co-founder of BirthVoice*

Dedicated to Baba,
the embodiment of Infinite Love

# Contents

# Preface

## The Story Behind the Book

This book emerged from years of working with mothers who have shown me what mothering means. Focused on the period from conception to the first or second year after birth, it is the heartfelt words of mothers from many different countries woven through the down-to-earth yet mystical path of Tantra Yoga. Peppered throughout the writing are bits of scientific research verifying truths that both mothers and Tantra Yoga have sometimes known for millennia.

From my time in the 1970s assisting mothers in giving birth at home to now, it has been a joy to observe women fall into the rhythm of motherhood and a joy to write down what they have taught me. It has been even more of a joy being an acharya or renunciate nun in the Tantra Yoga path of Ananda Marga since the early '80s. As a nun and therefore not a physical mother, I make no pretense to be sharing motherhood from personal experience. This is important for me to be clear on at the outset. That said, what I have experienced is a yogic way of life based on love for an Infinite Consciousness which is greater than any human love can ever be. I have understood that love on the human plane is meant to show us that love exists while creating a yearning for an even greater love. It has become clear that mother-infant love is without question one of the strongest examples of human love. I have observed how this love opens a mother's heart and mind and changes one's basic perspective on life in a very dramatic and visceral way. Itowards the biology of love was a revelation to me after some years to understand that mother-infant love is a profound partnership with the infant equally as powerful in experiencing and sharing love as the mother. And finally, the analogy of mother-infant love to the relationship of each human with the Divine became more and more apparent to me and ultimately, important enough to write about.

But it didn't end there. Other understandings have influenced this writing, some of which are:

- Standard birth practices tend to disregard the fact that the mother-infant relationship is, first and foremost, a love story
- For many reasons, pregnancy, birth, and infancy all too often fall short of the dignity and the joy these experiences are designed to bestow
- The mother-infant dyad was and still is a major evolutionary factor for the human species
- Infants and small children need to be more acknowledged in their contribution to the mother-child partnership
- And finally, the innate qualities of cooperation and respect embedded in mother-infant love are the qualities so needed now on the planet

## Who Are the Mothers in the Book?

Seventy-five mothers from different countries agreed to be interviewed with questions about pregnancy, birth, infancy, the mother-infant partnership, meditative or spiritual practices, and overall motherhood in the primal period. The countries represented are: Australia, Brazil, Colombia, Croatia, Cyprus,

Egypt, England, Estonia, France, Greece, Israel, Italy, Jamaica, Japan, Korea, Lebanon, Malta, the Netherlands, Russia, Serbia, South Africa, Taiwan, Turkey, and the United States. Some of the mothers were meditators and some were not but all were pursuing spirituality in their lives. I am deeply grateful to the mothers who so willingly gave their time for this project. What impressed me was the intensity and vividness with which most mothers recalled these times in their lives, even up to 30 or more years later. And additionally, how happy they were to talk about it. That said, the stories and thoughts shared were of a deeply personal nature and thus, to respect the privacy of the mothers, their real names have not been used in the mothers' quotes.

## A Few Words About Mothering Before Moving On

Although in this book we are speaking mainly about birth mothers, most of what is written applies to whomever is in the relationship of mother or primary parent figure. Infants ideally need a main figure or figures in their lives to whom they are most bonded, particularly in the first few years after birth. Any number of people may be the mother or main person. It is the qualities of mothering that are universal and not the specific parameters of motherhood.

## The Spiritual Base

The Tantra Yoga presented here is the philosophy of Ananda Marga propounded by its founder, P.R. Sarkar (also known as Shrii Shrii Anandamurti). Tantra means "that which liberates the mind from dullness by expansion" and yoga means "to unify". Dullness refers to the ignorance of what we truly are and why we are here.

Expansion from dullness means the realization of and ultimate unification with Infinite Consciousness. Both are aimed at moving the mind from the finite to the infinite and are used in this book singly as Tantra or Yoga, or together as Tantra Yoga.

Tantra was the spiritual practice of the indigenous peoples of ancient India which, over time, became influenced by Vedic and other philosophies and morphed into various spiritual schools of thought. The spiritual principles in this book are Tantric in origin, based on introversive practices and a fundamental guru-disciple relationship. At the same time, they incorporate more historically recent Yogic teachings. The result is a contemporary, doable methodology and philosophy for the 20th and 21st centuries.

The influence in my life of P.R. Sarkar, or Shrii Shrii Anandamurti, on this writing is so vast, it cannot be adequately expressed. The presence of such a guru or guide in life is a great blessing. He embodies the Infinite Love we are all seeking and acts as the means to make that love accessible. Thus does the concept of an intimate internal relationship with the most Beloved become real. It is my hope that any insights gained through this book will support mothers and people everywhere to keep the realization of this greater love as the foremost priority in life, to make regular committed efforts to actualize it, and to use what is gained to create, as Sarkar says, a "bright future" for all.

## Chapter I

# Mother-Infant Love

*To love: how perfectly our hearts are made for this!*
*Sometimes I look for another word to use but in*
*this land of exile, no other word so well expresses*
*the vibrations of our soul. Hence we must keep to*
*that one word: love.*

St. Therese of Liseux

## Partnership & Promise

"Call Kristina to come over!"

There are already seven people in the room singing to Margarita and her baby while they labor in the birthing pool, but she wants more. Margarita comes from a culture where the gathering together of close family and friends is a prerequisite for comfort in almost any situation. She is having a homebirth and nothing could be of more support than her women friends and her husband around her, melodiously chanting and filling the room with a quiet charm. A singer by love and profession, Margarita's throaty voice melds effortlessly with the rest, sometimes getting louder during the peak of a contraction and often softer during the pauses in between. In the early evening, an alert and curious baby girl emerges to the enveloping rhythm of the yogic chant, Baba Nam Kevalam, that has filled the room and everyone's senses for the ten hours of labor. The Sanskrit words, colloquially meaning

"The essence of love is all that exists", are an appropriate welcome giving credence to the heart force behind birth and life. The newly born baby is named Joy, with a middle name that means song. She is a song of joy.

Margarita and Joy's lifelong journey of love has begun to unfold. Their togetherness is the center of life for newborn Joy and will have an indelible impact on how she perceives love in her lifetime. At the same time, the relationship has the potential to expand Margarita's sense of what love is and how it is expressed.

The bodies and minds of both Margarita and Joy are inherently made to work together in unparalleled synchronization. This is particularly true in the period from conception through the first critical years after birth. From the level of physiological co-regulation to the extraordinary rhythmicity of emotional and behavioral interaction, a multilayered partnership has begun. This inbred harmony characterizes a particularly contemporary Tantric concept called 'coordinated cooperation.'

> Where cooperation is between free human beings, each with equal rights and mutual respect for each other, and each working for the welfare of the other, it is called coordinated cooperation.
>
> P.R. Sarkar, *Cooperatives*

It may seem outlandish to apply the concepts of "cooperation between free human beings … each working for the welfare of the other" to infants who are indeed totally dependent on adults for their survival. Our premise, however, is that in terms of shared love and its biological, emotional, and spiritual implications, infants are full partners in this relationship. The infant's love is as powerful as the mother's. Mother and child each profoundly influence the other, albeit from different levels of developmental awareness. "The idea that babies are in partnership with us," noted Zoe, a mother of three, "reframes everything we think we know about parenting an infant."

> Almost from the beginning of pregnancy but certainly from the second trimester onwards, I was so aware of my baby and I being in this together. I didn't feel like it was only about me carrying a baby. In some sense, I understood that she was carrying me as her mother. My daughter is now 10 months old and this feeling is still here, though it changes at times. I have to say that it has influenced me greatly in how I relate to her.
> Elisa

> I talked to my son a lot during pregnancy and I knew that he heard me. I understood even then that I would do anything for him and he would do anything for me.
> Arianna

The input of the child, and especially the infant, is often considered to be far less than that of the adult. However, the infant is far from a passive recipient. Her senses are wide open and she communicates in all the ways she knows how in response to those around her. Facial expressions, verbal sounds or cries and body language are obvious means of communication, but other signals are more subtle and could be described as intuitive. While biological reflex causes the infant to react instinctively, it is awareness from a more spacious mind that expresses itself intuitively.

Yogic science understands this intuitive subtleness to be a state of mind closer to pure Consciousness than the intellect and the emotions. P.R. Sarkar calls it an attunement to the universal rhythm, the collective vibrational essence of life. He asks the question, "Who does not like the spontaneous joy of the innocent faces of children?" and goes on to attribute this joy to the invisible spiritual link between unit (individual) rhythm and universal rhythm. The younger the child, the stronger is this link.

The hidden beauty of this aspect of an infant's mind is that it has the potential to be an exceptional gift to the mother, starting even during pregnancy. "There is a selected new ethic for me," observes Zoe, "that comes out of realizing that babies are very sensitive, very intelligent, and very connected with the universal life stream." Quite by necessity, the mother learns to communicate by developing her sense of intuition. On deep levels, the infant is teaching us much through the inherent silence of her being.

> A mother's intuition really grows a lot. She's intuitive about when her baby is well or not well. She has intuition about other things beyond her and her baby, things outside of her and her family. I don't know how to explain it … it's a sense.
>
> Lavanya

Intuition, in its broadest sense, is the conduit for realizing our connection to Infinite Consciousness. When the mother is aware of this connection and consciously cultivates it, her child's connection to Universal Consciousness is reinforced. The reinforcement in the child in turn strengthens the mother's awareness and a potentially lifelong feedback loop has begun.

Herein lies what may be the ultimate crux and purpose of mother-infant love. Mother-infant togetherness is inherently sacred in its design. As one of the strongest examples of human love, it begins long before a mother holds her newborn in her arms, long before she feels her infant moving in her womb, and long before she consciously or unconsciously ever thinks about having a baby. This love could be said to have begun with the beginning of existence as we know it, when life sprang forth from its primordial source, initiating the never-ending cycle of birth, life, and death. Each time a woman carries an infant within her and each time an infant comes into the world, they are re-enacting the very birth of life itself. As the infant grows within, emerges from and thrives in the care of the mother, so all of us live within, emerge from and thrive in the care of a Consciousness or a Love that is the source and core of all of creation. The realization of this inherent relationship with Consciousness, which the mother-infant relationship parallels in human form, may be the most far-reaching purpose of mother-infant love, and indeed, of love in any form.

Let's begin at the beginning and look at the roots of human love as we know it.

## Mother-Child Love & Evolution: Where It All Began

> Love requires warm blood. Warm blood causes warm feelings and warm blood is a very "new" invention in evolution, being only about 150 million years old. It was brought into the world by mammals, the last family to appear on earth and to which we belong.
>
> Ada Lampert, *The Evolution of Love*

Selam, a fossilized early human ancestor discovered in Ethiopia, may have spent part of her days walking upright on the dusty soil and the rest of the time in the trees with her mother to avoid predators. Living slightly more than 3 million years ago, her body was probably not much more evolved than her chimpanzee relatives. Her bones show us that she only lived about three years, not unlike the high percentage of other children of her era who most probably didn't reach maturity. Still, it's possible that her chances of survival and her quality of life were greater due, at least in part, to one factor — her mother.

It all started for Selam, and the rest of us, millions of years ago with the appearance of mammalian mothers. Signaling an evolutionarily massive shift from our reptilian ancestors' lay-the-eggs-and-run behavior, these mothers were the first to show the desire and ability to care about another's well-being as much as or more than their own. By the time Selam came along, her nurturing could have included not only breastfeeding and close physical contact with her mother, but also deepening emotional bonds, "talking" via primitive sounds and gestures and perhaps even a rudimentary empathic ability to understand nuanced, non-verbal communication.

Nonetheless, life was rough and keeping children alive was no easy task. Over the years, hominid mothers and infants both refined their skills, following the subtle yet powerful magnetism that evolved between them. By the time modern homo sapiens appeared on the scene, the demands of this growing relationship had given rise to the appearance of more sophisticated capabilities in the mother, such as a fierce sense of protectiveness, patience, resourcefulness, empathy, and a growing ability to tend to her children's needs before her own. This resulted in children with enhanced cognitive and emotional skills, who were more adaptable and resilient and far more likely to live until adulthood. As Leslie Meek, professor of psychology at the University of Minnesota, states, "The evolution of mother love was essential for the evolution of intelligence."

That the mechanism of intense mother-child attraction was designed to enhance infant survival is unquestionable. But the ensuing attachment, reward, and pleasure that became deeply grooved into our physiological and psychological fibers ultimately defined itself in the human mind as love.

> The conclusion (from the empirical data) is that human love evolved on the basis of the mother-infant relation ... with the growth of self-awareness, perception extended more and more profoundly into the self of the other. Love derived its first evolutionary importance from this.
>
> Robin Allot, *Evolutionary Aspects of Love and Empathy*

As time went on, the mother-infant relationship acted as the foundation for increasingly complex social relationships. Mothers and their offspring both developed ever subtler perceptions of self and others as they began to recognize themselves as part of a family and a community. Elaborate neural circuitry evolved dedicated to yearnings for love and belonging, as well as the capacity to fulfill those yearnings.

Evolutionary researcher Ada Lampert points out the uniqueness of human love in comparison to emotional attachments in most mammals and even in most primates by the breadth of objects we direct our attention and affections towards. "Human preeminence over chimpanzees is in the expansion of love onto more and more objects, not just mother and child but also man and woman, kin, friends, god, books, art ..." As our ancestors' human intelligence and emotional bonds continued to broaden in scope, intricate and diverse cultural expressions sprang forth from the vast resources of the human mind and heart, creating civilizations that have formed and shaped who we are today.

# The Bigger Picture: Universal Love & Social Change

> Human beings ... will have to accept the great
> responsibility of taking care of the entire universe.
> P.R. Sarkar, *Neohumanism is the Ultimate Shelter*

Our challenge at this time in history is to expand love even further, transforming human love into universal love in our own lives while simultaneously shaping society. Universal love exemplifies the transformation of awareness from 'me and mine' to 'us and ours'. Respect, cooperation, and sacredness are qualities at the foundation of this emerging evolutionary shift. Nothing can be left out of the picture — no human being, animal, plant, or inanimate object. "When the underlying spirit of humanism is extended to everything, animate and inanimate, in this universe," Sarkar explains, "this is Neohumanism. Neohumanism will elevate humanism to universalism, love for all created beings of this universe."

As the mother-infant relationship heralded an enormous evolutionary shift in the past, so it continues to offer itself as one of the foundational templates for this evolutionary jump. Amongst the multitude of human relationships we may have in a lifetime, that of mother and infant is where 'you' and *I* are the most closely connected, where we feel the other to be a part of us. Since all of life is about relationships, the relational construct of mother-infant love holds within itself the potential for a far broader connection with everyone and everything as next of kin. We are moving towards an ability to hold all created beings as dear to us as our own children. Really dear to us, not just as a lovely concept but as a reality in our gut and heart. "The love of your child extends beyond the physical being," writes Zen priest, Kyodo Williams. "Our heart touches the expanse beyond our own limited self and lets us know in a very palpable way that I'm not just this self. I'm all of this."

There are two essential and complementary aspects to the transformation of human love into universal love. One is personal and the other is social.

The personal side of love's realization is discovered in the stillness of a transcendent love that lies in the deepest recesses of the heart. It will never be found in misty-eyed, heart-palpitating romance, physical gratification, or even enduring, long-term affection. As undeniably crucial as all these human expressions of love are, there is no person, place, or object that can ever fully satisfy the innate longing for happiness. The significance of human relationships lies in the awareness of them as reflections of a love far greater than any human love can ever be. "Infinite love," says Sarkar, "is the ultimate expression of finite love." The depth of love between mother and child, when purposefully and methodically directed to its Infinite Source, may open new doors on the journey to a boundless sublime love. "The relationship with Consciousness is deeply intimate," observes historian and educator Marcus Bussey, "and the intimacy of the mother-infant bond is where it starts."

The social side of this expanding love allows for an evolving sense of ourselves as people committed to radically transformative social visions. It understands the very fundamental truth that one cannot personally progress without others progressing as well. As Bussey notes, "Spirituality ceases to be selfish and becomes a collective act." Caring relationships become the fundament of personal, social, economic, and political structures of wholeness. "This is the time when we need to create social systems," writes Riane Eisler in *The Way of Partnership*, "that support rather than inhibit our enormous biological capacity for caring, for consciousness, for empathy — all the qualities that we so need now."

We have become humans who care, sometimes passionately, for the groups we identify with. But it is the lack of true empathy for those whom we consider as 'other' that is an overriding cause of wars, environmental degradation, accumulation of wealth and resources for a few while many live in poverty, and so on. As Kyodo Williams so aptly states, "We have to make the structures of society unwilling to bear separation as a way of approaching things." The emerging social vision then becomes what Sarkar, in his extensive outline for a rational social system (PROUT or the Progressive Utilization Theory), describes as the inner meaning of the word society, i.e., *to move together.* "Building anything on humanistic lines requires a foundation of real love and affection for humanity," he says. "The basic ingredient for building a healthy society is simply genuine love."

That said, the transformation of human love into universal love is a huge task, one which requires all we can muster in insight, determination, and perseverance. It won't come about through wishful thinking or fanciful theories. Rather, it requires interweaving the rationality of the intellect and the sentiment of the heart with the systematic use of time-tested methodologies for expanding internal awareness. We are primed to experientially incorporate into our lives *intuitive* means of observing the world, which bring together the inner and the outer, self and society, and a personal subjective approach to life with a constantly evolving objective adjustment to the outside world.

> The nature of mind, consciousness, and reality as well as the meaning of life can be apprehended through an intuitive, unitive, and experiential form of knowing. The development of this type of consciousness is absolutely essential if humanity is to successfully solve the global crises that confront us and wisely create a

future that benefits all humans and all forms of
life on planet earth.

Maurice Beauregard & Denyse O'Leary, *The Spiritual Brain*

Tantra Yoga is just such an introversive, intuitive science
marrying intuition to logic, compassion to the intellect and the
heart to the secrets of the universe.

## Tantra Yoga in a (Very Small) Nutshell

There is spiritual force in each and every living
entity. The practical interpretation of Tantra is
to awaken this spiritual force and expand it,
with the one objective of unifying it with the
Supreme Divinity.

P.R. Sarkar, *Tantra and Its Effect on Society*

Tantra Yoga is both a spiritual science and a path of the heart.
Stemming from the practices of the indigenous peoples of the
Indian sub-continent many thousands of years ago, Tantra Yoga
was and still is a practical, experiential journey of self-realization.
Based on the understanding that an Infinite Consciousness exists
from which life as we know it emerged, our journey is to gradually
recognize Consciousness within ourselves and within all of life.
The ultimate goal is to merge our limited sense of self with limitless
consciousness, thus returning home to that Infinite Source.

As a methodical, intuitional science, Tantra Yoga is practiced
in the laboratory of the mind. The depth of its extensive
philosophy, outlining how the mind, body, and all of creation
work in conjunction towards the goal of self-realization, is truly
imbibed only as a result of direct personal experience. Tantra Yoga

is said to be 99 percent practical and only 1 percent theoretical. In other words, the knowing is through the doing.

This requires effort. These efforts are called *sadhana* in Sanskrit. Sadhana includes not only a philosophy to guide one through life but also regular practices such as meditation, sentient diet, yoga exercise and service. It also requires continuous motivation to maintain the efforts. Fortunately, the very nature of Consciousness supplies the motivation. As awareness expands, we are carried into subtler, more joyous, and more purposeful realms of existence. We understand more and more the truth that everything in the created world is interconnected. The closest word we have in any language to give a name to such experiences is love. Humans are made to love and be loved. Once we begin to access a love more expansive than human love, we go on making the effort because we want more.

It's important to note that Tantra Yoga is not about any particular god or goddess, nor does it imply a divine entity existing in heavenly realms to whom we pray for favors. Anyone who sincerely aspires for union with the Infinite, who does spiritual practices aimed at realization of the Great is a Tantric.

> Every sadhana that aims at the attainment of the Supreme, irrespective of its religious affiliation, is definitely Tantra. Tantra is not a religion. Tantra is simply the science of sadhana.
> P.R. Sarkar, *Tantra and Its Effect on Society*

The greatest of all love, and that which gives depth to human love, is union with the Divine. When experienced, this Love permeates everything in our lives. It is not about escaping from the world but rather about seeing the beauty in it. The world becomes both an expression of Infinite Love as well as a means of knowing it. All of life appears ever more beautiful and precious, prompting us to relate to it more deeply as our own. Its beauty feeds our soul while our soul feeds its beauty. Its pain stirs our heart while our heart longs to soothe its pain. Thus is the rhythm of love established.

The world as we know it, however, is impermanent. It can never be the final goal. It is the permanence of Infinite Love that inescapably pulls us. While the duality of life will always show itself as pleasure and pain, the immutable inner resource of infinite joy remains as the ultimate truth.

> This quinquelemental world has been born out
> of joy, is being maintained in joy, and into
> sacred joy will melt.
> P.R. Sarkar, *Vrajagopála and Aesthetic Science*

You might now be thinking, "Well, that all sounds very nice but how does it connect to mothers and infants?" Here's the connection: if everything is Consciousness or love, life itself carries love's signature. By looking through intuitive eyes at the design and the patterns of life, we get glimpses into the Consciousness that created it. The mother-infant relationship and birth itself reveal incomparable insights into love and joy. And through that, we may be guided into the Infinite Love which has enduringly signed its name on all babies, all mothers, all fathers, and all of creation.

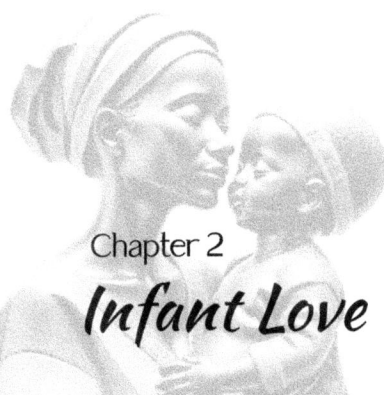

## Chapter 2

# Infant Love

*Babies are more capable than expected. They come bathed in mystery, genius wrapped in swaddling clothes, wearing their baby disguises.*
David Chamberlain, *Mind of Your Newborn Baby*

## The Infant's Enigmatic Mind: Spacious & Sweet

Infant love is a consummate mystery. It brings wonder and awe into the lives of adults, intriguing parents, inspiring poets, and stimulating researchers to design ever more sophisticated and subtle means of understanding the minds of our littlest ones. Some theories say that infants are little more than instinctive animals needing adult direction to guide or control natural impulses. Others point to social, relational, or cognitive influences as being dominant factors in who the infant is. There are those that emphasize the biological side of a new being, manifested in the breathtaking growth occurring from the moment of conception. And some remind us that the entire history of human evolution repeats itself endlessly in the embryonic formation of each new human child.

All of these factors reflect part of the complex picture of human life. While it is clear that infants are grossly incapable of maintaining themselves on their own, do operate reflexively from instinct, and are unquestionably influenced by people and places around them, this does not preclude the existence of an expanded awareness that is nearly, if not totally, impossible for the adult mind to understand. Most theories of infant development "view the child as emerging from *less into more*," writes Thomas Armstrong in his work on childhood spirituality. "Assuredly, these perspectives leave something out." While the child is certainly developing cognitively and physiologically from less into more, on another level, which can only be called spiritual, the child may come with access to intuitional or unconscious realms of awareness which recede over time from "*more into less.*"

> If we look at children as whole beings, we see they are very spiritual. In a holistic view of children, only their minds and bodies are undeveloped. They are spiritual beings, perhaps closer to a knowledge of God than we are.
>
> Jody Wright, *Parenting from the Heart*

What is this spiritual realm that infants, even before birth, and young children live in? The explanation is as elusive as it is real. Tantra Yoga notes that the infant's mind still lives within the spaciousness of the 'universal rhythm.'

> Every animate and inanimate object of creation emanates its own vibrations – the mighty mountains, the flowing rivers, the lovely forests. None is mute, none is silent. All are resounding with an inexplicable eternal vibration, as if in deep meditation. The collective rhythms of all the rhythms … is called "universal rhythm".
>
> P.R. Sarkar, *Individual Rhythm and Universal Rhythm*

Thus is the infant mind imbued with the sense of being seamlessly part of all that exists. The breeze, the light, objects, colors, sounds, and sights are all as alive as the infant or young child himself, not in imagination but in reality. On a deeper level, the infant's spiritual awareness understands that Consciousness is not only that which inhabits every cell of its being but *is* every cell of its being; that which orchestrates movement, growth, and form while at the same time *being* movement, growth, and form; and that which constantly changes, metamorphosing into body parts, senses, feelings and expressions, while simultaneously remaining *unchanged and constant.*

Sarkar describes this innate connection to Consciousness as a special kind of sweet, child-like bliss. Because there has yet been little worldly input in the infant's mind, the subconscious remains calm and tranquil allowing waves of bliss from the unconscious mind to easily surface.

> From the beginning every created being is situated in bliss. The very moment a newborn infant opens his eyes upon the world, he feels a type of bliss. The earth's light and air infuses a wondrous feeling of bliss in his mind. Not only a human child, every newborn being feels this certain type of bliss from the start.
>
> P.R. Sarkar, *The Means to Save Oneself from Sorrow*

This bliss may be at the root of what Alison Gopnik, an infant researcher at the University of California, calls spiritual intuitions. The minds of infants and children are steeped in a sense of awe and wonder, according to Gopnik, that comes from feeling connected to everything around them. She describes infant awareness as "a kind of exaltation and a particular kind of happiness." We cannot help but observe how happily infants interact with others or how children recover from an accident or an upset and begin easily playing again as though happiness is their default mode. That happiness is designed to be infectious, a kind of magnetic charm attracting the mother to the child. A friend recently said, in a very quiet and almost reverent tone of voice, "Just their smiles light up your life."

I suggest that infants and children have two main tasks in life: one is to work furiously hard to understand the world while developing the brain and bodily systems needed to live in it; and the other is to share happiness and give love. Let's look at how they do the latter.

## Infants: A Lot of Love in a Little Body

> Every baby comes into this world with the expectation and need for being loved. At the same time, every infant is primed to give a love that so often surprises mothers in its intensity. A mother who is listening with inner ears and feeling with an inner heart can learn of love from her infant.
>
> Anonymous

"One interesting question," writes author Naomi Stadlen when discussing the shared love between mother and infant, "is who teaches whom to love?" An often overlooked aspect of the mother-infant relationship is that it is a two-way street with the baby's love being as strong and potentially life-changing as the mother's. "We now know that children influence their parents as much as parents influence their children," notes Alison Gopnik, commenting on how much has changed in the past 30 years in terms of understanding this phenomenon. "After all, babies are a source of enormous intimacy and joy and meaning."

Author Penelope Leach goes a step further by asserting that, "Nobody else in the world including your partner, however devoted, is ever going to love you as much as your infant will in these first few years if you let him (or her)." She describes a feedback loop created from loving a baby who loves you back which makes you feel more loving … and on it goes. Romy, a mother of a small infant, confided that before having a child, she had heard that a mother experiences an unconditional love towards her baby unlike any other love. She went on to say that while that was certainly true, what people never talked about was the love a mother feels *from* her baby. "She's so small but her capacity to love is enormous!" Romy's words were tumbling out of her mouth as she tried to explain. "My daughter is always happy to see mommy and she accepts me in every mood I'm in, immediately and fully. I've never felt so much love before."

A mother of an infant and a toddler, Rene's experiences were strikingly similar to Romy's. "It feels so good when I look down at my baby and he smiles up at me as though he's been just waiting for me to do that." Or when she walks through the door and her 2-year-old runs up to her. "Their love is so strong. They love me ridiculously. It feels incredible."

The totally non-judgmental love from an infant may open a mother's heart and mind to hitherto unrecognized qualities. "From her baby, a mother can discover how it feels to be completely accepted by another person," says Stadlen. "Her baby may help her to recognize and to value the genuine good in herself." An example is Carmen, a woman who says that for years, she was afraid of becoming a mother. Her husband wanted children, but she struggled with the idea. After her daughter was born, Carmen realized that although it was enormously hard, she could do it. "For me, it was a very big step to have a baby," she says. "It was my daughter who brought out capabilities in me I never knew I had."

Additionally, infants and children may intuitively and compassionately understand the needs of their mothers far more than we ever imagined. "Babies can show startling sensitivity towards their mothers," Stadlen tells us. "They can be passionately warm." Anat confirmed this by describing how she, as a first-time mother, became quite depressed soon after the birth of her son, Jahi. He seemed to be aware of this and did his best to help her. When Jahi was only weeks old, Anat says, he began smiling at her. He would look straight at her and beam. She had him with her all the time and she began to notice such an awareness in his eyes. "He was speaking to me."

> Whenever I was depressed or hibernating, when I didn't want to talk or see anyone, he would look at me and smile. My reflex was to smile back at him. He was forcing me to smile. Especially when I was not in a good mental state at all he would do that constantly. And he only did it with me. Everyone noticed. My husband noticed. My friends noticed. He was completely in sync with my emotional state and his purpose was to balance that out. He gave me so much joy, he was the only thing capable of giving me joy. And I'm a skeptic. I'm a scientist and I really battle with spirituality and rationality. To see things that I can't explain in a tangible way is really hard for me.
> Anat

Rhea relates that with her first pregnancy, she had this tension that was, at least in some ways, connected to the fact that she was at first pregnant with twins but one of them died at 20 weeks. She went through a grief process after that, talking to the baby who was still alive, telling him she was so sad and at the same time, so glad that he was okay. Rhea always loved dancing and danced a lot for the rest of the pregnancy "but in a different way. It was so intense, this dance," she remembers. "My son came through the dance. I could feel it was the baby doing it. I could put into words only much later that I was not myself dancing but dancing with him. He was dancing with me."

The crux of the matter is that through the power of their love, infants, before and after birth, and small children have the capacity to be stabilizing, motivating, and proactive participants in relationships with others, particularly with their mothers. Our task as adults may be to recognize and acknowledge their input more fully. A heartfelt example of this came from a group of Syrian refugee women in Greece talking about the hardships they had endured living through war and being forced to leave their country. During a pause in the conversation, they were asked if they felt their babies and children helped them in this difficult situation. Without hesitation and almost with one voice, they immediately replied. "Of course," one said, "When I sit with my daughter or take her on my lap, I feel lighter. It helps me forget my problems." Another added, "They fill me with joy and make everyday life a bit easier." And a third continued with, "It's their love. It makes me feel stronger."

## Conversations with Babies: The Art of Listening

Actively and compassionately listening to an
infant isn't much different than listening to a

child or an adult. It requires empathy, genuine
love, and respect for the infant's experience.
Vimala McClure, *Path of Parenting*

When Artemis returned home after her first day back at work
since giving birth, her three-month-old daughter, Leah, was in
tears. "She's been like that a lot today," the babysitter said, and
Artemis's heart ached. Artemis herself had been near tears at her job,
the fast-paced TV industry being a far cry from the stay-at-home
mothering she had grown to love. "Oh, agapi mou (a Greek term
of endearment meaning 'my love'), agapi mou, come to mama."

Before Leah was born, Artemis had assumed that after three
months at home, she'd be quite ready to get back to her
demanding but interesting career. Leah had changed all that.
Artemis loved mothering her daughter more than she'd imagined.
For weeks before returning to work, she was distraught and did
everything possible to ease the separation. But being apart was
very hard for both of them.

"Oh, you're so upset," she cooed to Leah as she moved into a
quiet room where the two of them could be together without
being disturbed. After a few minutes of holding her gently and
looking into her daughter's eyes, she continued. "I know you're sad
and angry and so am I. It was awful for me, as well. You want me
to be home here with you and this is just where I want to be. We
miss being together so much." By this time, Artemis was also
crying. Leah's crying had changed from howling to big gasping
sobs which became less and less until she was unruffled enough to
steadily return her mother's gaze. "I don't want to leave you. I love
you so much." Their conversation went on like this, each deeply
communicating to the other.

Telling this story in our weekly infant massage group, Artemis
tried to explain to the other mothers what she had felt. "At that
moment, when she stopped crying and looked at me, our hearts

were like one. I cannot describe the magnificence of that moment. She had needed to cry. I also needed to cry. We did it together and really listened to each other. We were both so upset but there was the feeling that we would find ways to make it better." She went on to say that if we had not talked about listening to babies in our previous meeting, she would have undoubtedly done everything possible to shush Leah's crying with "Shh! Shh! Don't cry. It's all right." But the truth was that Leah needed to cry and be heard and when she was, Artemis said it was miraculous.

Most of us as babies were shushed when we cried, lovingly but firmly told to stop, that there was no need to cry, and so on. When this happens and there *is* indeed a need to cry, we learn very early not to trust our instincts or acknowledge emotions. Vimala McClure, founder of the International Association of Infant Massage, realized early on that the only problem infants have is not being listened to. "Infants need to be heard as much as anyone," she says. "I have seen many remarkable instances in which an infant's responsiveness and general disposition has completely changed after truly being heard." Babies have as much to talk about as we do. They need to vent emotions and have their feelings received with love and acceptance.

One of McClure's experiences was with a mother of a premature infant. "I don't know what I'm doing wrong," the mother said. "He just seems to like the babysitter more than he likes me. He is so happy and calm with her, but at home with me, he cries all the time." She had begun to feel negativity towards her baby and began letting him cry for long periods alone in his crib. McClure told her that babies in day care often save up their negativity, fears, and anger for their mothers with whom they feel safe. It was a demonstration of trust on his part, not alienation. This simple understanding changed the whole mother-infant relationship. Mom was able to go to her son with love again and listen to his troubles. Her personal power as a mother was restored and this enabled her to give beyond what she had been perceiving as her limit. The baby's crying began to diminish as he started to feel heard.

An infant massage instructor, Kylie, had this story to tell about a first-time mother and her five-month-old son. The mother was concerned because her son had not yet rolled over on his own and was showing no signs of wanting to. The pediatrician said everything was fine, but she was worried. Her anxiety was making the baby anxious, creating a circuit of nervousness between them. "We talked about listening to babies," Kylie related. "I suggested that she gently encourage her baby to roll over, but also tell him that she felt fine to wait until he was ready." She needed to calm herself and realize that babies are all unique and reach different milestones in their own time. The mother went home and tried it. As she was speaking to her baby, he started crying. Instead of panicking, she held her infant and soothingly told him that she was here for him in his distress. He cried for half an hour. She rocked and comforted him, telling him that he must have some deep upset and she understood that he needed to let it out and it was all right with her. After that, the exhausted baby fell asleep. When he woke up, he spontaneously rolled over.

Often, the reason for an infant's crying is not clear. She may be stressed from too much stimulation or anxiety in the environment. Infants and small children are aware of everything around them at once, something adults can no longer do. A baby will be hearing sounds, smelling the cooking aromas from the kitchen, feeling the softness or harshness of the sheet under her, watching the play of light on the wall, and enjoying the last tastes of milk in her mouth all at the same time, giving equal attention and importance to it all. This is one of the reasons why infants and small children become so easily overwhelmed by external stimulation. All their senses are on high alert and active input every waking minute.

Or he may be crying from a memory of upsetting events from pregnancy, birth, after birth or, per yoga philosophy, even from another lifetime. One mother said that her infant cried often around 4:00 pm and she found it very hard to settle him. I asked about her birth. She replied that labor went very well but when her baby was born, he wasn't breathing. There ensued a frightful period while the doctor and midwife worked on him. In the end, he was fine and they bonded well. Then I asked her what time he was born. She paused, looked at me with widening eyes, and slowly answered, "4:00 pm."

Whatever the cause of crying may be, an infant's cry can be very hard for mothers to bear. Because mother and infant are so deeply connected, she feels baby's laments viscerally in her own body. And though parents may love their children very much, an infant's cry can subconsciously bring up unresolved pain in adults who themselves were not listened to as babies. "I believe that the reason it is so difficult for us to listen to our babies," says McClure, "is that our own infancy may have been full of frustration and unheard feelings. When we hear our infants cry, rather than truly listening to what they say, our overwhelming impulse is to quiet that baby."

Being able to simply be with another person in their distress or pain may be challenging. It is, however, an irreplaceable gift to give to a child, or to anyone.

> I think that there's a lot of noise, external noise, that we listen to in terms of advice about mothering our babies, how to stimulate the infant's intelligence and so on. But making a space, a quiet, fertile space, lets things just come through.
>
> Zoe

Learning to make that quiet internal space to listen to babies not only strengthens mother-infant communication but spills over into communication with others. In the bigger picture, it reflects the greater conversation between one's self and one's higher Self. For most of us, refining our listening skills requires effort and mindfulness, both in the mundane sphere of life as well as in the spiritual arena. Given a chance, babies may be helping us to hear at deeper levels.

## Conversations with Babies: The Art of Responding

> When the mother is able to pick up the baby's communications, this is not a matching of behavior. It is more of an intuitive matching of their internal rhythms.
>
> Alan Schore, *What is the Self?*

The simplest of everyday interactions between mother and baby have deeply impactful consequences. The mother attunes herself to her infant's mind and body while the infant is attuning to hers. This coordinated cooperation, occurring on the most basic of biological levels, spawns an extraordinary physical, mental, and emotional synchronization between mother and infant.

> I found my moods affected by my daughter's moods. If she was playful or tired or cranky, I would pick that up. Maybe I reflected her moods. And I couldn't help but observe at times that she was reflecting mine.
>
> Magdalene

An amazing film clip I saw years ago captured the mother-infant synchronicity in a visually clear and beautiful way. The clip, part of experiments done at Boston University by William Condon and Louis Sander, showed an infant lying on his back while the mother's voice was heard though the mother was not seen. The arms and legs of the baby were moving in the seemingly uncoordinated stops and starts one expects from an infant. After a minute or so, when the clip shifted into slow motion, the mother's voice became the music and the infant, the dancer. The movements of the baby's arms and legs and indeed the whole body to some extent, were moving rhythmically and gracefully in tune to the intonation of the mother's voice. One could imagine the mother's voice unconsciously rising and falling in tune with the movements and gestures of the baby. It was as smooth as any choreographed dance could ever be and breathtaking to watch.

Added to this, the same study found that infants develop a specific repertoire of movements locked in perfect synchronicity with mother's speech patterns as early as the first day of life. For example, every time a 'kh' sound was uttered by the mother, the infant might move his head slightly to one side; when mother came out with a "rh," the child's little finger might jump up a fraction of an inch. The experimental team were astonishingly able to computerize the infant's entire repertoire of movements to mama's voice. But the most remarkable part of the study took place years later when these babies were seen again as adolescents and adults.

> The researchers discovered the subjects' reactions to these sounds were exactly the same as they were previously and that these reactions were now part of the subjects' permanent motor-system responses which could only be measured on a micro-level and then only by sophisticated

computer equipment. Yet there they were: a slightly turned head at a kh sound or a microscopically wiggled pinky in response to rh.

Fine and Fine, *The Art of Conscious Parenting*

While both mother and infant are absorbing and adapting to the rhythm of the other, an often-misunderstood aspect of this synchronization involves periods of time-out. Babies will gaze, play, laugh, and coo animatedly one minute, only to turn their heads away and look uninterested the next minute. This often confuses adults who wonder what happened, did they do something wrong? Too often, the adult continues to encourage the baby to keep interacting. But far from anything being wrong, the baby is simply communicating as clearly as she knows how that she needs a break. She's overstimulated and is saying, "I love playing with you. Just give me a minute to calm down and if I'm not too tired or hungry, I may be ready to go again."

A mother learns, respects, and follows the infant's cues, interacting when he turns towards her smiling and giggling with wide, alert eyes. She also learns when baby needs to disengage by crying, turning away or frowning. In an active and alert state of mind, an infant under five months may initiate interacting and disengaging up to four times a minute. Though growth allows infants to engage for progressively longer periods at a time, this rhythm of play-rest-play-rest continues right up through preschool.

The seconds or moments of disengagement impress on both mother and baby the necessity, value, and beauty of retreating temporarily to quietness amidst activity. Infants are, in fact, showing us a law of life, that forward movement is always followed by a resting phase. This could be challenging for mama, who may herself be used to constant activity.

Many infants grow into children and adults who are uncomfortable with pause, silence and stillness. Both mother and baby learning to love the periods of pause will not only further synchronize their communication but go a long way towards helping them both appreciate the beauty of quiet times in life.

> The period immediately after a "moment of meeting", when both partners disengage, provides an "open space" in which both can be together, yet alone in the presence of each other.
> Alan Schore, *Effects of Secure Attachment*

As one mother put it, "I think if you stop for a minute to listen, quietly and calmly, the communication will be there in whatever form it takes." Periods of pause, stillness and quietness amidst activity are normal and essential parts of life. From sitting for a one-minute silence to regular meditation practices, the ways are endless. Our children are showing us that they need this and when we follow, we realize that we do, too.

## Stress & Balance: It All Depends on Joy

> What is important is to carry the child's mind along in the current of joy.
> P. R. Sarkar, *The Practice of Art and Literature*

"One evening after I gave my baby a bath, she started crying and wouldn't stop," recounts Tina. "That was when I took a deep breath and tried to make eye contact with her and help her find her center again. I understood that she just needed to cry. I held her and cried with her, and I could feel her relief. When she stopped crying, she let out a really deep sigh. It was an incredible experience for both of us."

What Tina was doing was being the ground for her baby's physiological and emotional states to come back into balance. Her baby was not neurologically able to do it on his own. Infants are not yet hard-wired to be able to control their reactions in highly stimulating situations, whether in excitement or distress, and can easily be overwhelmed by fears, survival instincts, and strong emotional feelings. Many people who were not helped as children to understand disturbing reactions have literally become adults with the same infantile responses. "Some adults remain stuck with the emotional development of a toddler," writes Margot Sunderland. "Because no one helped them enough with stress and distress in childhood, they never set up effective stress-regulating systems in their brains." An over-stimulated child throwing a tantrum without caring parental response may well become an out-of-control angry adult. Responsive mothering means mothers who understand this and bring baby back to his default place of balance and joy.

> She soothes loud crying and over-arousal by entering baby's state with him, engaging him with a loud mirroring voice, gradually leading the way towards calm by toning her voice down and taking him with her to a calmer state. She soothes a tense baby by holding and rocking. She stimulates a lackluster baby back into a happy state by her smiling face and bright eyes. By all sorts of non-verbal means, she gets the baby back to his set points where he feels comfortable again.
>
> Sue Gerhardt, *Why Love Matters*

The sweet joy of an infant's mind is the default programming. Mama's smiling face, bright eyes, and warm, loving touch provide the calm, joyous grounding that brings the infant back to that place, again and again and again. Psychologist Allan Schore calls this a matching of the minds and bodies, a sense of empathy in which "someone's body is exactly resonating with my body". Gradually, the child develops the essential brain pathways to enable him to calm himself. "Unconsciously we pick up that skill," says author Kathy Brous. "After we cry and mom comforts us for the millionth time, one day we feel our way to stop crying because we've internalized her comfort. Mom was an external object, but now we've taken her image inside us, so we feel loved and emotionally secure 24×7, even when we're alone." Love has become a real, visceral, and accessible experience.

The deeper purpose of mother-infant resonance, however, may be to prime us for the joy that knows no bounds, cannot be described, takes lifetimes to cultivate and fills our hearts and minds to overflowing.

## The Ultimate Joy: A Larger-than-Life Love

> Trials and tribulations compel people to ponder
> deeply. Their wounded hearts want be soothed
> with a healing balm from an Entity greater than
> themselves. When the greenness of the world
> fails to moisten the deserts of their minds, when
> the seeds of their desires do not sprout, then
> they realize they have to go still deeper inside.
> The key to the solution lies deeper within.
> P.R. Sarkar, *Shivopadesha 1*

Infinite Love begins with having our hearts soothed and our minds calmed by a presence larger than ourselves. Tantra Yoga exemplifies Infinite Love as that of a parent with each of us the small child looking to a larger-than-life love for solace and comfort. And when we find it over and over again, we understand it as a purely internal joy. As time goes on and the depth and beauty of this love matures, we understand that, as mother-infant love is reciprocal, so is Infinite Love. What begins as receiving comfort and joy becomes giving comfort and joy to others and to the Infinite Entity behind it all.

The infant will learn gradually over the first few years that although mother truly is a part of himself, nonetheless she is also separate from him. The Infinite Self, on the other hand, is the blissful joy at the core of who we are. Once we have internalized that truth, we can never be separated from it.

# Mother Love

*I think that the love between a mother and her children is the closest possible. They are with me every minute. Something connects us even when we are not together. I cannot explain it really. It's not something to be explained through words. It's about the heart.*

Lien Hua

## Mother Love: A Unique Phenomenon

"The word 'mother' describes a relationship, not a role or a job description", says author Naomi Stadlen. Like any relationship, it is filled with contradictions. Heart opening and mind boggling. Enormous stamina and tremendous fatigue. Instinctive and yet a learned skill. Stormy days when mama may want to give the baby back and cherished moments when she's flooded with how precious it all is.

Mothering may indeed be one of the most formidable, under-acknowledged tasks in life. One mother summed it up in brief by saying, "It is the hardest job in the world with the least amount of training." Author and educator Ivana Milojevic notes that "Most if not all mothers I know find mothering challenging, exhausting, sometimes confusing, sometimes even traumatic, even while most agree that in the end it is 'worth it' and 'rewarding'." And Denise

Roy, author of *Momfulness*, honestly shares that, "I love being a mom, and at the same time, motherhood can be incredibly grueling and frustrating, pushing me to my limits."

"Motherhood can at times be suffocating, imposing or clinging," notes Aliyah, a first-time mother. "It can feel like a huge burden because your life is on hold, your life is secondary to the survival of your child. At the same time, you would do anything for this being whom you love so much." She stops speaking for a moment as though measuring the weight of her words. "This is not intellectual. It's what happens. I don't know if it ever goes away."

The magnitude of becoming a mother is so impactful, it doesn't happen overnight. Simply being happy to be a mother is just part of the picture. Having mother's and baby's bodies brimming with love hormones at birth or afterwards is only the beginning of the story. "Loving isn't automatic," writes Susan Kuchinskas in *The Chemistry of Connection*. "We have to learn how." This is true for both mother and baby. "Becoming a loving mother is not an inevitable result of having a baby or being flooded with oxytocin," notes Naomi Stadlen. "Only we ourselves can make our love happen." It takes time, patience, and effort to learn what this love is about.

"I didn't immediately fall in love with him," recalls Erin after the birth of her first child. "I loved him, but I didn't feel that immediate rush. I felt excited but not really like a momma. When he got his heel pricked and I held him and I was the only one who could calm him, that's when I felt like a mother. It's not what you imagine beforehand, and when you don't feel like how you think you are supposed to feel, it's almost scary."

Sophie is a first-time mother of a three-week-old girl. "I never had contact with a newborn before I gave birth," she says. "I worry if she's all right." Her voice is near tears as her story continues. "The night we came home from the hospital I was so confused and desperate, all I could do was cry. And now I'm getting so little sleep that I am exhausted." Sophie admits though that even in three weeks, things have noticeably begun getting better. She is gradually learning to read her baby and trust her instincts. She pauses momentarily, stroking the infant at her breast. "Still," she looks up as a smile spreads across her face, "I wouldn't trade this for anything. Underneath the worry and fatigue, I am so happy. She brings me so much joy."

No two mothers will experience mother-infant love in exactly the same way. From the very moment of conception, the trajectory of each singularly personal mother-child relationship begins to take shape. Each birth, each child, each relationship is unique unto itself. And yet, mothers everywhere express similar underlying sentiments about this most powerful of human connections.

> I was fine before becoming a mother but once I had children, I couldn't live without them. As soon as I became pregnant, I realized that if they were to not be here, I'd be devastated forever.
> Kiirana

> It's different from any other love. I am only concerned about her. It is about forgetting yourself to take care of another person.
> Magda

> It's unexplainable, the mother love. It's a strong protective feeling and joy and hope all rolled up into one.
> Erin

> You would do anything for this being, you'd put your life down, everything revolves around keeping that newborn well and healthy and

you are just completely enamored. It is so powerful. I wasn't prepared at all for what that was going to be.

Ayla

Mother's love is quite unique. Knowing someone from the very start of their life and watching them unfold in front of your eyes allows this sense of fascination or amazement or delight at how this person is emerging. The love and bond between you are indescribable.

Rafaela

The experience of love mothers feel during and after giving birth are often indelibly stored in their memories. When asked even many years later, most women recall it vividly and easily. They speak of a love that sometimes exploded like fireworks in their hearts and minds and sometimes crept in more gradually, like night becoming day in the early hours of dawn. It was most probably the same for the infant.

I don't think I felt tremendous love at the moment I saw my babies because the births were so painful and the feeling of relief was so strong. But the love was innate, and it gradually kicked in as I woke up from the shock of giving birth.

Karina

I was in awe each time I first saw the babies. It's truly a miracle, a process of love and intimacy. I don't ever lose that feeling. I look at them still with the same depth of love and the same sense of awe I had from their births.

Miki

When he was born and I saw him, I had no feelings except extreme tiredness. That night I was dreaming that I held my son on my shoulder and felt such a love and closeness for him unlike I had ever experienced before with anyone. And when the nurses brought him to me, I was really very happy and in love.

Valyn

My first birth was long and difficult, and I lost a tremendous amount of blood. Losing a lot of blood had made me a bit woozy and I was not so glued to the baby at first. It took maybe 12-24 hours before that incredible mother instinct really kicked in. I can almost remember the moment when I suddenly felt it and from that moment, it was total.

Alexandra

Both my births were cesarean. I was awake though and my babies were put on my chest immediately after birth. It's a moment you never forget. I remember that I cried. Even with a C-section which is an operation, I immediately wanted to take care of my child. It was so natural.

Sabahat

It really hit me when I started dreaming about
him. Then I knew I was a mother.
Erin

"You love these children more than anything else in the world.
If they get physically or emotionally hurt, it's deep in my heart, it
hurts me more than I could ever have imagined." Rhea's words,
an attempt to describe the indescribable depth of a mother's love,
are echoed by mothers everywhere. "But the truth is that we
could lose them at any time through sickness or death or
something horrible could happen now or when they are grown.
We have totally given our heart to something impermanent and
not fixed at all."

You're doing it not knowing if it will ever be
given back to you. I may get sick sometime in
the future and they may not be taking care of
me in the way I take care of them now. Being
aware of all that, not knowing what could
happen and still pouring out the love as much
as you can is what mothering is about.
Rhea

Learning to love, to quote Eric Fromm, is an art. We are not
talking about the emotions of love which sometimes sweep
through mother and infant but rather the steady flow of a deeper
current, not always obvious but always there. Rhea recalls that
before her father died, one of the last things he said was "It's all
about love." She goes on to say that you hear people say things like
this all the time but then somehow one day, you "get it. You really
get it. You realize you've learned to stop, to listen, and to trust."

# Mother Love & Spirituality: What's the Connection?

> The moment of birth connected me to the
> timeless experience of every mother in human
> history who had gone through this miracle of
> giving birth to another human being from her
> own body. That in itself is quite cosmic and
> when something miraculous happens, it takes
> you out of mundane life, mundane thinking
> and makes you feel a part of all that is.
> Ramona

"The creative nature of the experience [of pregnancy and birth] may lead to a greater awareness of 'something beyond' the earthly realms," writes author Jennifer Hall. Midwife and birth activist Robin Lim takes that a step further by noting that "Birthing is the most profound initiation to spirituality a woman can have." Pregnancy, birth, and mothering push mothers to their limits and beyond while opening the heart to love in often unprecedented ways. This carries within it the potential to change one's sense of spirituality or bring forth something that was not there before. "I didn't have a concept for that greater spiritual essence in life before my first child was born," says Zoe. "I think it was something in him that brought that out in me. I felt so deeply still. It wasn't a conscious decision. It was just the way it was."

> In the years following the birth of my children,
> my spiritual growth was much more than it had
> ever been. It helped me to start looking at what
> it is that I'm feeling and how it translates onto
> a grander scale.
> Maia

Mothering and the deepening relationship with God went hand-in-hand. I never thought about the connection and am not sure if it would have happened anyway, but mothering is certainly something that brings that up.

Mahi

Having a baby is a miracle. It's a process of love and intimacy, a whole sense of creation beyond the self, truly the hand of God. I may not be aware of this at every moment, but I don't ever really lose that feeling.

Maire

Becoming a mother is a very wonderful and mysterious process that brought me closer to my spiritual self.

Margot

My spirituality has become more grounded since becoming a mother, more real in some ways. It's not as other-worldly. I used to see more of a separation between the experiences of meditation and everyday life, where meditation is real and the world was kind of annoying and not that interesting. But those differences have narrowed. Spirituality has become more real and practical.

Kate

The practical expression of spirituality shows itself as the gradual transformation of human love into universal love. Mothers could be said to be primed for universality because of the enormous love which has overtaken their lives. Motherhood holds the possibilities of expanding this love to include all people and everything in creation. Quantum physicist Danah Zohar notes that when a mother's whole being feels inseparably interwoven with her infant, it accentuates the ability to see the connection between things. She sees this as a deeply feminine perspective, made very real through motherhood. It is a step to universal love. "I realize now that this is how I'd like to love everybody," confides Themis, a mother of two. "How I feel about my daughters is how I want to feel about everyone. This love is teaching me that."

> I loved children before having my own. I am a schoolteacher and work with children every day. But after giving birth, I love them even more, all the children.
>
> Marina

> I always cared about the environment and have been actively involved in environmental issues for many years. But after becoming a mother, I feel even more strongly about it. I feel an urgency to pass this feeling on to my children and to all parents and all children.
>
> Sara

> After birth, I was seeing people with a lot more compassion. No matter what they did or had ever done to me, I looked at them and thought, "This person is my child." It changed the whole way I thought.
>
> Dahari

> I think mothers, when they are true to
> themselves and aligned with motherhood, have
> in their hearts the intention to be a mother to
> all children and all people.
> Kris

Sarah Napthali, in *Buddhism for Mothers*, calls mothering a huge step towards 'the mind of love' and very rightly speaks of the unbounded potential it holds. "Through loving a child," she says, "we deepen our capacity to be a loving person for others too. The potential to take what we've learned from loving our child and apply it to other relationships is limitless."

## Mother Love: A Stepping Stone to Divine Love

> Just as God signifies unconditional love, so does
> a mother for her children. In this way a mother
> prepares her child for an intimate relationship
> with God.
> Vandana

Does mother-child bonding and early childhood nurturing have an influence on our relationship with the Infinite Source of being? Does a loving, caring environment make it easier to bond with a Divine Love?

A very emphatic 'yes' to these questions echoes through an impressive research paper from the Commission for Children at Risk (CCR), a collaboration of neuroscientists, medical doctors, and social scientists in the field of children's mental health. According to their findings, the quality of early primary relationships does indeed set the stage for spiritual development. Their premise is that "Human beings are biologically primed to seek spiritual meaning. Nurturing relationships are a central foundation for positive spiritual growth."

"The earliest faith is the basic trust and hope in the care of others," write Ross Thompson and Brandy Randall in *Children's Spiritual Development*. "A caregiver's nurturance, protection, and availability provide the basis for the earliest grasp of divine care." Constancy, trust, and sensitivity to needs are requirements as well as outcomes in both loving human bonds and bonding with a spiritual Entity. As Dr. Paul Zak tells us, "Belief in God depends on trust ... trust between individuals are the same mechanisms needed for trust in God."

For an infant who emerges into an unknown world, the mother is initially the main guide in learning how to trust the world, to trust that care will be given and love will be returned. "The deep-seated, ferocious, universal love of the mother begins and fortifies the soul's journey throughout life and beyond," explains Margot, a mother of two and a preschool teacher for thirty years. Expounding on the spiritual relevance of this love, she speaks with the voice of one who knows these truths from personal experience. "The mother's love (or parents' love) is the physical representation for the love of the Divine in our lives."

While there are many factors influencing one's relationship with a Higher Power and attributing it solely to a mother's or parent's care is an oversimplification of a complex process, it is intriguing to wonder how much relates to early relationships. The neuroscientist Andrew Newberg quotes a survey from Baylor University wherein the participants' perceptions of God ranged from a fearful authoritarian or critical figure to a very distant entity with no emotional connection, while for some, it was a God who cares, listens, and responds. "We remember how important people in our lives feel about us not in words but in our bodies, emotions and images," says psychologist Todd Hall, who has interviewed hundreds of Christian college students about their spirituality and early life experiences. "This shapes how we feel about ourselves, God and others."

Thus, a mother's loving touch and responsive, open heart may allow the child to conceptualize the love and responsiveness of a Supreme Entity, a Universal Mother. A father's playful stretching of the child's body and imagination may prime the child's psyche to attach to a loving Infinite Father who stretches and carries us beyond our seeming limitations. And the warmth of the home has the potential to be recreated as the inner home away from home, the ever-present solace of Love in the deepest caverns of the heart.

## Mothers & Dharma: Motherhood's Ultimate Purpose

> Experienced as a powerful love, mothering holds within itself deeper insights into life and may carry a mother further into truth and purpose than she would ever have imagined.
> Aliyah

Dharma means innate characteristic or that which sustains and drives a living being. The dharma of the sun is to be the nucleus that holds the solar system together. The dharma of a plant includes growing, nourishing the soil and giving off oxygen. The dharma of mothers is to open themselves to love, giving their children the chance to slip into that opening. Mothers commit years of their lives to nurturing others, losing sleep, being on duty 24/7, putting others' needs before their own, giving solace and sharing joys, learning patience, compassion, and humility … in other words, opening to love. Mothering is one of the external expressions of dharma.

You have chosen to be a parent because it is an important aspect of your purpose on this earth. What I know without any doubt is that bringing every gift I came here with, every iota of strength and wisdom, every drop of love and loyalty, everything I have to the task, the mission, and the gift of bringing up two souls to live their own lives and fulfill their destinies is the most important thing I have ever done or ever will do.

Vimala McClure, *The Path of Parenting*

Mothers instinctively want the absolute best for their children. Most agree that no matter what happens down the road, they hope their children will be happy. Tantra Yoga understands that the desire for the deepest, most constant, and sustaining type of happiness is the basic characteristic of living beings and pulls us constantly.

The dharma or characteristic of an individual is to lead his or her mind from the finite to the infinite, from a part to the whole. This characteristic emanates from the urge for happiness. So long as the object is not limitless, eternal happiness cannot be achieved.

P.R. Sarkar, *The Call of the Supreme*

In humans, our innate drive to find happiness is ultimately fulfilled only by the realization of our deepest Divine Self. The very purpose of living is to know what we are. "We have got to know that inner self," says Sarkar. "Knowing oneself is the true dharma, our true nature, to know who we are, where we have come from."

Since unborn and newborn infants as well as small children live within the subtle layers of the mother's mind, they are enveloped by her internal awareness and external actions. Thus, the infant's connection with the consciousness of the Great is inextricably intertwined with the mother's connection with the consciousness of the Great. The dharma of motherhood may boil down in a nutshell to cultivating this connection.

> What comes to my mind when we talk about mothers and dharma is distilling love so that it is more refined, more subtle. Learning to do that.
> Felicity

> A mother's dharma is to be in an intuitive relationship with her children enough to be able to fulfill her own dharma and create the atmosphere for them to be able to do the same.
> Rhea

> Mothers and dharma? It's about love. That's the nature of mothers. The essence. Why is that important? Because love is the most important thing in the universe. The purpose is to nurture these new beings with love.
> Alexandra

The kind of commitment to mothering that is stirred through a mother's love is the type of commitment to dharma that is stirred through the experience of Divine Love. Once having tasted its sweetness, determination to merge Divine Love into the very fiber of our being becomes a driving force to which we have no choice but to be committed. It is this purpose that may be the most important aspect of motherhood and that gives a sense of direction to the child. "Nothing one does with an infant should be purposeless," wrote the Sufi master, Hazrat Inayat Khan. "There are many who after they are grown-up cannot accomplish a certain purpose in their life. Very often the reason is that from their childhood, when the forces were rising, they were not directed to a purpose."

> Being a mother has made me question what life is about. I truly search now for the meaning of life so that, hopefully, my children will do the same.
> Yvonne

> Motherhood creates a real sense of purpose. To raise children who will be themselves and at the same time, to heal the planet.
> Niovi

> My pregnancy with my son made me realize that I am here in this life for a greater purpose. I found myself knowing on a deep level that this greater purpose is reflected in everything I do, the people around me, my job, and so on. I am more conscious of what I do, why I do it and what's important.
> Maire

This purpose, of course, does not preclude but rather underlies the cognitive, emotional, skill, and task-oriented capacities necessary for the child to develop. The world will teach children cognitive skills, but it takes sensitive mothers, fathers, teachers, and others to transmit the heart qualities of kindness, cooperation, intuition, and compassion.

Children have an innate spiritual nature. It's either fostered or squandered. At a very young age, my daughter was very interested in God and love and she was very empathetic. When she saw a child on the street without shoes, for example, she'd begin to cry. One of the most real parts of mothering is to hold onto that and not desecrate it.

Maia

Sadhana (practical efforts towards realizing our oneness with Infinite Consciousness) can and ought to be started in childhood, according to the child's age and capacity. Vimala McClure, the founder of the International Association of Infant Massage, says that children of all ages, even infants, can be spoken to about dharmic life. With older children, opportunities abound to talk about dharma in relation to events at school, something a friend said or did, TV programs, or a new app. But with infants who cannot converse in words, their extraordinarily uncanny ability to grasp inner meanings lets the import of the words soak in.

The baby "gets it" when her mother responds to her with love. A mother can speak to her infant about anything, and it might seem like an infant cannot understand. But I believe that babies understand and take in what mother thinks and says if it comes from deep inside her.

Vimala

"Remember always that you are not your body nor your intellect. You are a pure being, an expression of Supreme Consciousness." So chanted the renowned Indian saint, Madalasa, to her children from before birth and after. Her songs conveyed subtle truths that she wanted them to grasp in their innermost minds and hearts. "As long as you think you are but a child in a small human frame, you are spiritually ignorant. When you realize that you are a part of the Supreme, you become that Supreme." Her heartfelt words were aimed at impressing on the minds of her children that they were not just physical bodies, personalities, thoughts, or feelings but something far deeper, greater, more loving, and more expanded than the limited sense of self. Seeking to maintain the purity of the infant's being, Madalasa sang to infuse their minds and hearts with the will and capacity to follow dharma. Her children, as the story goes, grew into wise and enlightened people.

Though modern mothers' words or expressions may be different from Madalasa's, the intention to realize dharma remains constant throughout the ages. "We have to find the essence of what this life is for," said a mother of two, "so that our children can find what their life is for."

## Dharma Unfolded: Expansion, Harmonious Flow, & Service

> In order to know everything, you know one thing. That one thing is dharma. That one thing is the supreme truth and that truth is hiding in your heart. You have got to know that truth inside yourself.
>
> P.R. Sarkar, *Dharma Sadhana*

The extraordinary aspect of humans relative to animals or plants is twofold: first is that we know life offers us more than transitory physical, material, mental and emotional achievements; and second, we have the capacity to set our sights on and reach the greatest possible "more," the realization of Self.

Social neuroscientist Jaak Panksepp tells us that 'seeking' is the most basic and broadest of the biological brain systems. Though it deals with seeking to satisfy physical requirements like hunger and thirst, it is also activated in searching for meaning and purpose. This bundle of nerves and chemicals wants to find out what life is, what can be done and then move into "Let's get up and do it!" mode. It's a kind of "can-do" system which animals in laboratories will push levers to experience again and again, even more than for food.

This seeking is the basis of dharma. Seeking is a word of action. It is not just liking or wanting or even longing for something. It implies acting to get it. No matter what happens, we will always seek food, shelter, clothing, company, good feelings, and the like. And when we get them, we stop and enjoy the meal, make our homes our castles, delight in family and friends, and revel in love, excitement, adventure, and joy. And when the pleasure of the moment is but a memory, instinctively we want it again. But looking for lasting joy in anything impermanent and transient is a futile endeavor. Sarkar tells us that, "Everything has a limit, but human longing and thirst are unlimited. With limited objects, unlimited hunger cannot be satisfied." Following dharma entails training our minds to move towards the experience of a blissful, inner love, letting it pull us towards itself again and again.

How does our dharma drive us towards self-realization? Through three components: Expansion, Harmonious Flow, and Service.

Expansion of our hearts and minds takes many forms. Some are subtle, some more obvious, but all are designed to stretch our awareness towards the greatest possible love. In Sanskrit, this biologically built-in quality of expanding is called Vistara. As Sarkar says, "Vistara (expansion) is drenching one's human values and existential awareness in a flow of sweetness and expanding that throughout the universe." In other words, imagine the sweet joy of mother-infant love, expand it exponentially an unlimited number of times and one may begin, only begin, to come close to Infinite Love. It is, however, through finite experiences that we may catch a glimpse of the Infinite.

A mother of two confesses that when she was pregnant the second time, she wondered if she would be able to share her love equally with her two children. Her daughter, then four years old, absorbed her love so totally that she simply couldn't imagine how it could be spread two ways without being diminished. She realized after giving birth that her love was not at all stretched or lacking. Rather it felt doubled in quality and quantity. With awe in her voice as she told this part of the story, she said that she experienced more love with two children than with just one.

> Mothering exposed me to the world in ways I was not exposed to before, opened my eyes to sights and sounds I was not aware of, to subtleties I never noticed, subtleties in people's words and actions and even in my own words and actions.
> Diana

> Becoming a mother expanded my way of looking at the world. I could no longer think of just taking care of myself, or my husband and myself, or even just my family. Everything and everyone became very precious to me.
> Yvonne

Research fellow Michael Towsey, in his book *The Eternal Dance of Macrocosm*, compares this aspect of dharma to the inborn, never-ending urge for growth without which living organisms, ecosystems, and the biosphere itself would not survive.

> Motherhood pushed me to grow, to find out
> who I am and what life is. It gave me a different
> perspective, helping me connect to creation, to
> all the powers and beauties of life — not talking
> about it but experiencing it.
> Eliora

The second aspect of dharma, which seems to conflict with expansion but actually complements it, is referred to by Towsey as homeostasis or *harmonious flow*. Known as Rasa in Sanskrit and literally meaning *flow*, it is equivalent to striving for balance in the midst of constant growth and change. "Growth necessarily implies change and creating new structures while homeostasis implies preserving an existing delicate equilibrium," says Towsey. "Life will always strive for homeostasis but not quite achieve it because growth will always intervene."

Like expansion, harmonious flow keeps us on our dharmic path because of the underlying joy. Sarkar explains Rasa (flow) as "being saturated with ever-blissful awareness – to enliven human existence with sweet freshness. This becomes possible only when one maintains a constant link with the Supreme Entity from whom one's individual existence has emerged." As a mother's heart is always connected to her children, the link with the Infinite is even greater, sweeter, and enduringly constant throughout all of life.

These two dharmic characteristics are designed to work in exquisite partnership. The growth principle, or expansion, allows us to be open-ended, creative, flexible, adaptable, and just plain interesting. It's our in-breath, our heartbeat, waking up in the morning, giving birth and being born. While growth is seeking, homeostasis is integrating. Homeostasis, or harmonious flow, makes space for pause, assimilation, insights and understanding. It is breathing out, the heart in fleeting nanoseconds of rest, going to sleep at night, and the joy after birth.

Pregnancy and birth are two of life's supreme examples of this balancing act. A masterful play of mind-boggling expansion occurring within two organisms simultaneously, pregnancies succeed due to an inner intelligence, a profound undercurrent of love maintaining a flow, or equilibrium, amidst the changes. When a mother, during the unrelenting surges of giving birth, is able to fully give of herself and surrender to the experience, expansion and flow become one. On a deeper level, expansion and flow reach their zenith when one aligns oneself with the Infinite so much that the borders disappear.

As the heart's voice becomes louder and clearer and easier to hear, a third quality of following our dharma emerges. Service, or Seva in Sanskrit, is a natural attribute of mothers. In fact, it is a natural attribute of all humans but has the potential of being developed to a high degree in mothers. Seva means not just giving or taking care but going the extra mile, over and over again and feeling good about it. Even more than feeling good, Seva feeds our souls and carves our characters.

> Parenting as tapah (the yoga value of service with sacrifice) is the ultimate sacrifice, to give yourself to another person. Sacrificing in extreme can turn into masochism and neuroticism. In balanced form, sacrifice brings awareness.
> Kate

Tantra Yoga paints the picture of caring for our children as manifestations of the Divine towards whom we are humbled and grateful to be able to serve. This does not mean glorifying our children or raising them to the status of deities. It means connecting with their hearts and being fueled continuously by the exchange of love. It necessitates conscious effort to remind ourselves of the beauty of the moment; to create times of quietness, no matter how small or how challenging that may be; to step back and see the big picture of how fast these children grow and how precious these moments are, and ultimately to affirm again that it is the longing for the Great that is our deepest desire. With practice, the efforts become habits.

> I can't tell you how many times I would sit for meditation and my son would come over and sit on my lap and I'd spend my meditation massaging my son who I would ideate on as being Consciousness Itself. I was not massaging a small boy but the true Greatness that he is in his soul. And I was being massaged back, receiving the touch of that Greatness.
> Kate

> I think that I am serving God in the form of my child and that everything I do should be like that. Everything is part of an integral whole. I think motherhood has been a major factor in realizing this.
> Mahima

> Now that my children are grown, I often suggest to young mothers to make conscious effort to look every day at their babies and see the beauty and the miracle and just feel it.
> Emunah

Seva is not confined to our own immediate families. The challenge of transforming human love into universal love pulls us to greater and greater arenas of action. "I passionately believe that a motivation to serve something larger than ourselves – our families, communities, students, employees, customers, humanity, the environment, future generations, and life itself," says Danah Zohar in the *Spirituality in Education Newsletter*, "is the highest form our spirituality can take."

My friends and I decided we would join a food buying club in order to get good, clean veggies while supporting a local organic farm. We had all thought about it before, but it took becoming mothers to give us the incentive to do it. We not only became more aware of what our children would eat but realized we wanted to pass on to them the awareness of how their food came to them. At the risk of sounding fanciful, I felt like I wanted to be kind to another mother, Mother Earth, to take care of her more deeply than I had felt before.
Diana

We became actively involved in starting a progressive school in our area once our son was born. It may sound selfish that we only did this for our own son, but it wasn't really like that. It was more the fact that his presence made me deeply feel that all children deserve a good education. When my son was grown a bit and before I had my second child, I started volunteering in a program for less advantaged children whose parents couldn't provide them with a quality education. I don't know if this would have happened if I hadn't become a mother.
Valyn

> I have become a better person as a mother, for
> sure, both for myself and to help others. The
> strength I've received is to give back to other
> parents. When my 2nd child was about 6
> months old, I surprised myself by starting a
> parenting group. It just felt like I had to do it.
> Arianna

Dharmic mothering is not just about taking care of others but also taking care of oneself. Sometimes mothers give, give, give until they lose sight of the love. Dryness and burn-out come from the heart not being heard. Doing everything possible to take care of oneself, to find harmony and balance within, is as much dharmic service as caring for others.

> If I didn't get a lot back from my children, I don't
> know if I could go on. Still, even with that, I
> learned that I give but I have to give to myself
> as well.
> Arianna

Mothers who struggle unremittingly with overwhelm may feel terribly alone and isolated, which then engenders further feelings of inadequacy, depression, resentment, guilt, shame and so on. Most mothers truly love their children and want to enjoy them but are sabotaged by situations that may be unforeseen, develop insidiously and loom dismally insurmountable when they are happening.

Human beings are not designed to, "go it alone," most particularly when caring for children. Mothers need the company and support of other like-minded mothers. Finding or creating supportive networks is a dharmic service mothers can do for each other.

# Community Calls: Mothering the Mother

> Community is the spirit, the guiding light of
> the tribe, whereby people come together in
> order to fulfill a specific purpose, to help others
> fulfill their purpose, and to take care of one
> another. The goal of the community is to make
> sure that each member of the community is
> heard and is properly giving the gifts that they
> have brought to this world.
> Sobonfu Somé, *The Spirit of Intimacy*

Being in the company of other like-minded people is clearly
seen in Tantra Yoga as a basic necessity in pursuing a committed
spiritual life. This is so true as well for mothers and children.
Probably not much else compares to the 24-hour intensity of
motherhood, especially in infancy. As one mother said, "It's just
so easy to get lost!"

> First time mothers often feel insecure and need
> support. We need support and strength from
> husband, family, and friends.
> Miki

Nearly every mother I know unhesitatingly confirms the
need for community, emphasizing both the lack of it and the
often very intense effort it takes to create it. Statistics from two
American surveys show how astonishingly alone and
unsupported many mothers feel. In one, only 25-35 percent of
women felt that they received the affectionate, emotional,
practical, and enjoyable support from friends and family that
they needed. And in the second, 58 percent of mothers reported
loneliness, with 4 out of 5 saying they needed more friends.

I was very isolated for a long time. I was really happy to be with my babies, but I was alone. I was so excited to go to the La Leche League (a breastfeeding organization) meetings to be with other like-minded mothers. I went one day in a snowstorm, just assuming it was still on. It was quite a distance away and when I arrived, no one was there, not even the leaders. That's how desperate I was for other mothers' company.
Diana

I didn't feel any connection with other mothers when my child was young. I was very isolated. I'm sure I could have been less isolated but for many reasons, I didn't reach out to others. If I had to do it now, I would certainly do it differently
Myrto

I loved my son dearly and was very happy to be a mum but to be honest, I felt overwhelmed so much of the time. I had my children before the internet, so I didn't even have the chance for cyber company. I really felt alone.
Victoria

The emergence of nuclear families has laid enormous responsibility for childrearing on a parental couple. Sobonfu Somé, author and member of the Dagara tribe in West Africa, says that parents having the whole responsibility for whomever the child becomes "is a little bit too much to ask of just two people." Needless to say, this is even more the case in single parent families.

> I am convinced it takes community to fully
> raise a child. To be in your house raising a
> child while your neighbor is in her house
> raising her child is not normal. The way we do
> it in our society is not natural.
> Nalinda

Sobonfu tells us that in her native tribe, it is understood not only that "It takes a whole village to raise a child" but also that "It takes a whole village to keep parents sane." The sometimes extreme pressures a mother feels can create a whole host of cascading difficulties in relationships with her husband or partner, other family members, the baby or with herself. Many of these onslaughts could be minimized to manageable levels with the right sort of support from others.

> A friend came to visit and stayed one week. She
> had two children under six and so do I. I
> realized what a difference it made to mother
> with another woman. It seemed so easy
> compared to being on my own. We shared the
> days and the children. I miss her now that I am
> alone again.
> Marta

> I had a really hard time after my C-section, and
> I felt terribly alone. My husband would have
> loved to stay home but he couldn't. I was crying
> a lot. Fortunately, I had a few friends who came
> by and sat with me. They didn't do anything
> else but at least I wasn't crying alone.
> Kate

Sometimes mothers express that they wished they had made friends with other mothers or pregnant women before they gave birth.

> I wish I had started making community when I was pregnant. I live in my husband's country and it's a new culture for me. There are other mothers around me, and they are great mothers, but they think differently than I do. I am learning some things from them and yet I long for 'like-minded' mothers.
> Chantal

> After my son was born, I didn't know any other mothers with small babies, and I didn't seem to be able to meet any. I'm not a very outgoing person but if I'd realized how much I would crave the company of at least one other mother, I would have made more effort during pregnancy. I met pregnant women at the hospital and in classes, but I just didn't make friendships. I would suggest to new mothers to think of this when they're pregnant.
> Alisa

More traditional community customs have built-in mechanisms for sharing childcare. Grandparents, aunts, uncles, and cousins, as well as friends, neighbors, and the community at large provide a network of care, relieving and augmenting the attentions of the genetic parents. Having been dubbed names such as alloparents, the attachment ensemble, collateral kin, or cooperative breeding, these familiar adult caregivers and relatives are a vital part of children's lives. In some countries, in the immediate days after the birth of a child, the room or home will be filled with relatives and close friends, each taking their turn holding the baby and passing the newborn around. While this may somewhat or very much affront contemporary sensibilities of privacy, there is something of a traditional beauty to being welcomed into a family of many.

In the twenty-first century, communities take many forms. Seventy percent of mothers in one survey reported that they talked to other moms online. For some, these friendships fill a deep need as one in three confessed that they tell things to their cyber friends that they don't share with "real, physically pokable" friends. And nearly 34 percent of the mother respondents said that online friends became offline friends, often long-lasting ones.

Where on-the-ground mothers' groups exist, the logistics of getting to these meetings may be arduous, traveling across town hauling bags of baby supplies. Most mothers agree that the effort is well worth it.

> In my community, there were two mothers' groups that happened each week. We'd meet in the park or someone's home. There was a homebirth group and two playgroups and it made all the difference. It was a wonderful community.
> Kiirana

Two mothers who could not find such groups started their own.

> Together with a few friends, we rented a community space. We had a library of interesting books and had people come in and give talks on things of interest to mothers. We had to leave that community space and we went

through various incarnations, but it goes on in a subtle form. The friendships formed are solid and we still meet.

Ramona

I started a backpacking babies' group when my first son was about two. Every two weeks we met and went for walks in the forest with our babies on our back. It was a chance to talk with other women while we were walking.

Kiirana

Having a circle of mother friends is good, but even one friend can be the much-needed lifeline. One woman said that after her first child was born, she had a daily phone date with a close friend, also a new mother. Whatever was happening, they would make that call. At times, too busy or strung-out to talk, the conversation might be, "Sorry, I can't talk now. Good to hear from you. Talk later." And sometimes they would chat. It didn't much matter. They knew the other one was there and though they would also get together with the children, most often they would meet by phone. She said it was a life-saver.

I talked every day at 4:00 pm for years with my friend who had a baby about the same age as mine. It became a very supportive ritual. And it went on long after infancy. We talked together every day for six or seven or eight years.

Marcella

The blending of nuclear family circles with wider peripheral circles creates strongly needed communities, whether that community is urban or rural, living near or far, two or three families or twenty or a hundred. Cooperative relationships, between people and people, as well as amongst people, animals, plants, and all of life, is the only real ethic for a sustainable future. And it begins with mothers and infants.

## The Kaeshik Sentiment: Sentimentality as a Strength

> Women can perform extraordinary feats that men cannot. Had these potentialities been harnessed for constructive activities, there would have been many benefits for the world, but as this aspect of women's psychology is not known, society has not utilized their potential fully.
>
> P.R. Sarkar, *Sentimentality: A Special Quality in Women*

An intriguing and unknown concept surrounding women's potential is called the kaeshik sentiment and is connected to the characteristic of purposefully directed sentimentality as an innate resource and strength. I have found this topic to be one that brings up many questions and thus, before jumping into the heart of it, I will digress briefly to touch on thoughts often brought out by this discussion.

Kaeshik relates to emotions and sentimentality and the general female capacity to experience them more easily and perhaps in a different fashion than men. That sounds discriminatory to many people and both women and men can sometimes feel quite offended. The first point to be understood is that we are talking about female/male characteristics and not specifically about body type. Secondly, we are rightfully sensitive to this topic since, stereotypically, women and emotions are clumped together in a very negative light. A Forbes article on powerful women in business quoted a woman CEO as saying, "A woman who shows emotions in the workplace is often cast as too fragile or unstable to lead. A woman who shows no emotions and keeps it hyper-professional is icy and unfeminine. For many women, it can be a no-win situation." The problem is not that we have differences but that female attributes have been distorted and degraded for centuries and we have come to believe the distortions are true when they are not.

Women and men do differ but also, they do not. In a Tantra Yoga perspective, the differences are due to the inherent duality and complementarity of life and affect only mundane expressions and not the core of one's existential existence. Sarkar speaks of the slight edge that women have for sentimentality while a sense of systematic rationality is somewhat partial to men. The words slight and somewhat in the previous sentence are crucial because neither of these realms is solely the possession of only one gender and show themselves in varying proportions in all of us.

Sentiment and emotionality are an unparalleled source of strength. Extreme biological love maintained by deep, intense feelings may indeed be the heart fire that propels mothers to manage the inordinate physical and mental changes of pregnancy, to tap into the stamina and endurance needed for birth, and to tenaciously nurture growing children for many years.

> Evolution selected emotionality together with intensive motherhood. The emotions were and are a necessary condition to evoke the mother's behavior. In the same way that evolution selected milk glands, the womb, the birth canal and so forth, it selected the urge, the concern, the joy, and the satisfaction that motivate mothers.
>
> Ada Lampert, *Evolution of Love*

Several areas of the brain associated with emotion and love have been found to be larger in women, perhaps expanding gradually over millions of years of continuous mothering. Interestingly, some of these same brain areas which are innately larger in women seem to be activated and even increased in volume and size in both women and men by the regular practice of meditation. The anterior cingulate cortex, for example, connected with empathy and compassion and called the "true heart of the neurological soul" by Newberg and Waldman in *How God Changes Your Brain,* has been shown to be larger in women and to thicken in long time meditators. Perhaps women and mothers have a biological head start to meditative practice. Or perhaps the path of mothering is closer than we think to the path of expanded love.

Back to the kaeshik sentiment. The Sanskrit word 'kaeshik' means an extreme expression of emotion such as compassion, love, affection, or attraction, as well as repulsion, anger, shame, or hatred. Emotions experienced fully and strongly carry within themselves a powerful dynamism that has the potential to be harnessed and used, either to build or to destroy. Sarkar says that under the spell of kaeshik, "People climb the highest mountain summits, sail into the blue void, and touch the inaccessible poles." However, "Under the spell of kaeshik, one may commit suicide." Kaeshik sentiments are over-the-top emotions, those that are forceful and overwhelming. Like everything human, we are challenged to consciously use them well.

> People cry out in their extreme joy; they cannot contain their happiness within the narrow confines of their nerves. And in the case of hatred, even if they do not want to express it openly, neither can they keep it suppressed. People cannot suppress their overflowing

emotions of love, affection, compassion, etc., nor keep them under control. They must give vent to their feelings.

P.R. Sarkar, *Sentimentality: A Special Quality in Women*

Letting ourselves feel at such a deep level and fostering the ability to direct the energy appropriately is our challenge as potential kaeshik-ists. The down-to-earth requirement is a synthesis of emotion and intellect, a blending of female and male tendencies. Though the jury may still be out on the exact interplay between rationality and emotionality, it seems that they are so profoundly connected as to be dependent on each other for a full life. "Feelings are a powerful influence on reason," says Antonio Damasio, a longtime researcher into emotions and the brain. "The brain systems required by feelings seem to be enmeshed in those needed by reason." He goes on to say,

> Nature appears to have built the apparatus of rationality not only on top of the apparatus of biological regulation, but also from it and with it. Cognitive processes elaborate emotional processes but could not exist without them.
>
> Antonio Damasio, *Descartes' Error*

The obvious assessment would be that *rational sentiment* is best. Sarkar describes sentimentality based on rationality as the strongest force in the universe. Sentimentality, particularly strong kaeshik urges, have to be rationally guided towards an expression that truly benefits everyone involved.

As essential and powerful as rational sentiment may be in exploring the kaeshik urge, there is an even more basic motivational force needed to guide it to its greatest heights. Physicist Danah Zohar observes that "Neither reason nor emotions can appeal to anything beyond themselves. They have no transpersonal dimension." This transpersonal dimension has been called devotional sentiment.

## Devotional Sentiment: The Greatest Treasure of Humanity

> As long as devotion is absent, one's heart is like a desert; and when devotion is attained, an oasis appears in the desert.
> P.R. Sarkar, *Astitva and Shivatva*

When mother love has kicked in, mothers are devoted to their children. We use the word "devotion" when we mean a viscerally experienced, laser-like, all embracing commitment of love. Devotion is also a word used to connote the relationship of love between our individual self and the Universal Self. That relationship is just as real and changing and challenging as any relationship can ever be. Cultivating this love requires perseverance, sincerity, and regular, ongoing effort. But if the truth be known, it is far and away much sweeter, stronger, more tender, and infinitely more sustaining than any other love. The source of this devotional love is not dependent on any external conditions. It is purely personal and accessed from within the deepest, innermost corners of one's heart. As the Sufi poet, Rumi, so beautifully declared, "My Beloved grows right out of my own heart, how much more union can there be?"

Sarkar tells us that since ancient times, learned people have been accepting that the wisest person in the world is the devotee. Devotion implies listening to and following the deepest inner urges for fulfillment, forever directing one's awareness far beyond the materialistic and ego-centered world. Devotion inherently expands one's capacity to love to include an ever-growing spectrum of created beings and inanimate objects. It is devotional sentiment, when cultivated to a high degree, which carries within it the potential for raising existence to something sublime, not just for oneself but for all of life.

According to Tantra Yoga, devotional sentiment is "the highest and most valuable treasure of humanity" and must be carefully preserved. "Because it is such a tender inner asset," Sarkar asserts, "to preserve it from the onslaughts of materialism, one must build a protective fence around it, just as people put up a guard-rail around a small tender plant." He continues by asking the question, what is this protective fence? "It is a proper philosophy which will establish the correct harmony between the spiritual and material worlds and be a perennial source of inspiration for the onward movement of society."

Tantra Yoga's practical and yet mystical foundation in life provides a superb devotional base for the physical, mental, and emotional challenges that will always await us. But more than that, it opens a door for the realization that what we experience through mother love is but a tiny fraction of what love has to offer. And *that's* a staggering thought.

Chapter 4

# Mothers & Meditation: The Challenge and the Joy

*Life with children is naturally noisy*
*Can you find the silence within the noise*
*Can you feel the peace within the turmoil*
*If you cannot reflect in the chaos of the moment, withdraw*
*Make time for yourself to turn inward*
*Prayer, meditation and the like can help you stay centered*
*and aware of the deeper levels of what is happening*
Vimala McClure, *The Tao of Motherhood*

## The Many Levels of I: From the Mundane to the Sublime

"I birthed alone because the midwife and others didn't make it in time," recounts Sarah, a woman who had been doing regular meditation for years before giving birth. "If I hadn't been familiar with meditation, I don't think I would have had any frame of reference for what happened to me." The feeling for her was an intense closeness to the Consciousness of life, while at the same time being very much in the body and totally aware of all the bodily sensations. "You feel the body and the pressure and the exertion but it's not in the body, it's in the mind. The presence of that greater Consciousness is very strong and very real. It's a profound spiritual experience."

What Sarah experienced was a reality beyond her usual sense of *I*. As human beings, we see ourselves in light of what Tantra Yoga describes as different levels of our *I*-ness. The *I* of I want, I have, or I do identifies primarily with what we look like, what our strengths and weaknesses are, what we wear or what kind of house we live in…in other words, with our physical, material, mental and emotional selves. These levels of *I*-ness occupy us constantly, experiencing pleasure and pain and all the other drives of everyday existence. The underlying reality, however, is that a deeper level, the *I* of *I am* — or simply *I exist* — is far more sentient and powerful than the *I* of I do, I have or I want. This feeling of *I exist* is a subtler point of mind, a place of peace hidden within the incessant activity of all the other *I*s.

But *I exist* is not the end point. Like peeling an artichoke to get to its heart, yogis aim deeper. Beyond the mind itself is the experience of the Atman or soul, the purest reflection of Infinite Consciousness in our individual selves. And even deeper still is the dissolving of the individual soul into Infinite Consciousness. Our journey in life is to recognize and move through all the levels of existence, gradually refining the finite sense of *I* until it realizes itself as the Infinite *I*. Tantra Yoga meditation is designed for this journey.

> In order to realize the Supreme Perfection, a human being will have to give up his or her I-ness; that is to say, s/he will have to merge his or her petty I-feeling in the Great I-feeling. What is this petty I'? It is like a pot full of water in a pond. Now if the water of the pot is to be unified with that of the pond – actually, both the waters are intrinsically one – the pot intervening between the two waters has to be

removed. After the removal of the pot, there will
remain no distinction between the water of the
pot and water of the pond. Both become one.
P.R. Sarkar, *Vibration, Form and Color*

Tantra Yoga is clear that the everyday self exists as a relative
reality, a real construct within which we live. Who we think we are
and the world we live in are not illusions, but neither are they the
full picture of existence. They are simply the shelter and the means
for the incarnating mind to achieve its goal of Self-realization, for
the small *I* to move towards merger with the Greater *I*.

A car is useful to move us from one place to another. The body
is like a car, a physical form with a brain and a nervous system
through which the mind can express itself. The driver of the car is
the mind with its many *I*s. Without these physical and mental *I*s,
we would have no way to get to our destination. The soul is in the
passenger seat, silently navigating the trip. And the destination is
Consciousness itself.

Let's break that down in terms of the human infant. Babies
are certainly closer to Pure Consciousness than most adults. But
as infants, we have not yet figured out how the body and mind
work. The individual *I* feeling is only gradually appearing, taking
years to mature. The soul does a lot of navigating at this point.
The driver — the not yet fully developed cognitive abilities
which will gradually lay claim to the sense of 'self'— can barely
see the roads, let alone know which ones to take. As creatures of
feeling and intuitive spaciousness, infants lack a developed
intellect as a roadmap.

To harness the innate connection to Consciousness, we need
the faculty of self-reflection and the ability to direct our minds
consciously and consistently towards the desired goal. Infants and
toddlers are just starting to develop these capabilities. A two-year-
old may have an innate sense of rhythm and respond excitedly to

music but she won't be writing symphonies until her brain has matured. Spiritual focus requires the same kind of developed brain. Mothers have the capacity for meditative spiritual focus that infants lack. Because of the innate mother-infant connection, the mother's meditation may be adding a deeper, subtler direction to the developing mind of the infant. This may be the most precious gift a mother can give to her baby.

## The Bond of Silence: Listening from Within

> Consciousness is the conversation each element
> of this universe has with the whole. Ultimately,
> it is an expression of love.
> Marcus Bussey, *The Evolution of Consciousness webinar*

Love has the potential to create a kind of silent and deep communication between mother and infant. In western cultures, we generally don't think of communication in terms of silence. Silence holds within it a fullness and an expansiveness that requires inner ears to hear, inner eyes to see, and inner feelings to touch. The stillness that accompanies silence comes from the center of one's being. An infant is communicating much just by existing in that center. The mother is receiving and answering the communication, most of it below conscious awareness, through the embodied closeness that comes from the bond between them. It is a timeless meeting of hearts and minds. Carrying the memory of millions of years of mother-infant love and an infinity of Divine Love, silence speaks wordlessly. And what it speaks about are things that matter. The sound of silence is indeed the voice of primordial Consciousness. Ultimately, our minds merge with the silence of All That Is.

Every small or great action of your life
Every pulsing vibration
Is an eloquent language

Tranquil mountain ranges
Flowing rivers and streams
All are absorbed in an
Inexpressible sound of meditation

Only those with inner ears can hear it
None of these sounds is distinct from the
Cosmic Sound
From that boundless sonic manifestation
All are its inseparable flows

P.R. Sarkar, *Vibration, Form and Color*

For the mother to acknowledge, appreciate, and maintain this conversation of silence is a great gift to the baby, a gift that comes back to the mother as well. The small child rests quietly in mother's arms with no need for words. The infant looks into her eyes seeing not her face but her wholeness. If we don't try to fill all the spaces with actions or words, if we follow the child's cues, we can be led into a rhythm of life that naturally includes silence and stillness. Even a few moments throughout the day or at night before sleep or whenever it's possible, will reap rewards. Without this, both mothers and children can be left gasping for breath, wondering why life feels so frantic.

If you just settle down into a more still space,
then the silence of your baby talks to you. It is
a quiet heart space.
Zoe

And this, of course, is one of the bottom lines of why mothers meditate. For mothers who are busy every minute, who may be overwhelmed and tired, who may work outside the home as well as fully mothering within the home, the very thought of making time to sit silently or to practice meditation may sound utterly unrealistic. And particularly so when children are infants or preschoolers, still needing so much from their primary caregivers. And yet, mothers who find manageable and doable ways to fit it into their lives usually find the rewards incomparable. Let's look at how and why they make it happen.

## The Hearts & Minds of Meditating Mothers

> I cannot imagine living without meditation and
> spiritual practices in my life. They have added
> such a depth to my love. That's the simplest way
> I can describe something indescribable.
> Chloe

Mothers and yoga, mothers and meditation – do these thoughts conjure up images of a mother doing a standing yoga pose, gracefully holding a baby in one arm, and cooking dinner with the other? Or meditating in an immaculately tidy home while her children peacefully and quietly play around her? Or the mother who is always and endlessly patient, wise, and kind?

As comical as these idealized images may be, they underlie the basic premise that meditative practices are not about perfection in everyday life or days filled with Super Mama feats. At its simplest, it is about being able to come back to center when you've lost it, remembering your purpose, strengthening the capacity to listen to oneself and others, and setting priorities while letting go of the rest. About feeling good with yourself as a mother. And about incorporating meditative or yogic practices in whatever ways fit a busy mother's life.

"Meditation helped me with my parenting although my kids were aware of it more than myself," writes Buddhist meditator and author, Sarah Napthali. "Once when my daughter was visiting a schoolmate, her mother asked, 'Why does your mother meditate?' and my daughter's response was, 'Well, she's nice to be around and it looks like she feels better.' It was quite accurate. One of the effects for me was like waking up after being for a long time in a slumber state. I began to see how much I'd been on automatic. I also felt I'd found home."

We are all, in a sense, travelers away from home, lost in a foreign land. Our souls long for expression but our everyday minds keep us locked in the pull of the world around us. Tantric meditation understands that although we will always be taking care of ourselves and others in the necessities of daily life, there is a way to live more fully in the depth of the moment. And when we lose sight of it, which we routinely will, we know how to come back.

> On the practical level, what happens is that the unconscious mind is all-pervading, integral, and immeasurably vast. Through spiritual practices the riches of the unconscious mind are brought down into the subconscious mind. Then, according to one's needs, one is able to bring this acquired wealth of the subconscious mind into the conscious mind and use it in the external world.
>
> P.R. Sarkar, *Indukamala to Lyatta*

That all means experimenting constantly with how to gain and regain balance. "Life is a constant effort to restore an unstable equilibrium," says Sarkar. Outer balance will always be lost. That's a law of nature. As soon as your infant seems to have established a routine, she's teething or simply growing and suddenly the routine changes. Just when the morning rhythm of getting everyone out of the house on time seems to have found itself, one child decides he absolutely cannot go to school in these shoes, another forgot to tell you she has to be at school 15 minutes early, you can't find the infant's baby carrier and then the car breaks down ... it doesn't end. Expecting it to is unrealistic.

When outer balance is lost, inner balance often follows. The loss of balance itself is one of the blessings of life as it keeps us on track, motivating us again and again to be more honest, simpler, and more real. More accepting. More ready and willing to use the tools spiritual practices have to offer. The meditative mind is about going within even amid great challenges. A mind trained through meditation is more likely to give a vantage point from which to see harmony amidst the seeming chaos. Along the way, mothers may gain the ability, as educator and author Ivana Milojevic put it, to "reframe challenges into a spiritual practice, seeing the challenges as not only helpful for spiritual practice but as a spiritual practice in itself."

> Meditation brings you back to yourself. Even just 10 minutes gets you back to quietness, peacefulness, feeling centered. I keep telling myself that the chaos and the mess around me is temporary. They grow so fast and it goes so quickly. When I focus on this, I don't get so upset about the craziness. Meditation helps with this realization.
>
> Rhea

Meditation helped me be the kind of parent I wanted to be.

Dana

Yoga practices help me to become more patient. Before, I could easily get angry and wanted to control my child according to what was right for me at the moment. I wasn't thinking as much about what my child was going through. I tune in now to the way my child is feeling rather than controlling or pushing. I am giving space for my child and for myself.

Sevim

I cannot even imagine if I didn't meditate. It's like a medicine for me. I'd be insane if I didn't do it. It's incredibly easy to lose yourself... no time for showers, for brushing teeth...so easy. I can remember smelling like sour milk from breastfeeding and not having had the time to take a shower. I feel like I've given up a lot, not just my time but my old life. It's meditation that keeps my mind in perspective.

Renata

Amelia, a mother who strives to make meditative practices part of her life, realized something of this dynamic in one of life's commonplace situations. On an ordinary day when she was cooking dinner, her two children started arguing, ending with her younger child crying. As she went over and picked him up, the phone rang, the dog on the veranda started barking, her older child began crying, and she could smell the dinner burning. To her own surprise, she didn't panic or overreact. As though guided by a quiet, unseen instinct, she simultaneously took a good breath and turned off the stove, mentally blocked out the sounds of the phone and the dog, held her son, and came down to eye level with her daughter, calmly speaking to her. Within minutes, all was settled, the children were back playing and even the dog had mysteriously stopped barking. And it had seemed easy, almost effortless. Though Amelia is the first to admit that most potentially explosive situations don't run such a smooth course, she knows her intuitive sense is deepening, her center of calm is strengthening, and she is gradually but surely moving in a flow ever nearer to her heart's being. And when situations do explode or the chaos is overwhelming, she is kinder to herself.

Tantra Yoga stresses, however, that this kind of clarity does not happen only by wanting it. It requires thoughtful and persistent practice. This practice is called sadhana. Sadhana is a word used colloquially to mean meditation or striving to merge one's mind with the Universal Mind. In its fullness, however, it implies the concentrated and practical *effort* to attain realization while keeping balance amongst all the aspects of life, inner and outer.

One is never at the point where this effort isn't needed. A rock climber may have great skills and know-how, but they'll be of little use if she doesn't keep her awareness fixed on the sensations that make up each moment of the climb. Each climb. Every time.

> I realized that you need to keep practicing even during pregnancy or when the children are small, even if it is less. You can feel a quiet internal space more easily and not lose balance so quickly if you are practicing regularly. For example, even when you get mad or lose your temper, doing practices helps me calm down

easier and go to explain or talk to my child about what happened.

Sevim

Most mothers agree that with the demands of caring for children, creating meditative space requires ingenuity and purposeful intent. Some mothers can do twenty minutes or more of meditation regularly once or twice a day, though many of those who do, have either meditating and/or supportive partners or helpers.

> I never missed my meditation even when the boys were small. I was very lucky because I have a husband committed to meditation so there was never a question about that. Also, he worked at home and he could do it and he was willing. We just took turns with the children to let the other do meditation.
>
> Kris

> My husband helped me. When he came home from work, he took care of the girls, and I could go do meditation.
>
> Mei Ying

For many mothers, even with this kind of support, meditation takes on a different rhythm. The point is to be adjustable while keeping to the intention to incorporate meditative times into the day. A long-time meditating mother of four frankly recalled that each time she had a new baby, her spiritual practices went down. "I eventually came to accept this," she said. "I realized that guilt can actually do more to prevent moms from spiritual growth than lack of time does." She and most mothers feel that the key is being flexible — and feeling good about it.

I needed meditation to feel sane after she was born. I just did meditation whenever I could. For example, I might do 5 or 10 minutes, sometimes many times a day. When I made the effort to do that, I felt so blessed and the meditations were so good.

Noriah

I had been meditating for so many years that I could not stop but I could not do as long as before. When I had one child, I did longer but when I had two, it was shorter.

Lien Hua

I don't meditate as often or as long as I used to, but I still do regularly. I sit by her bed or do it when she is relaxed. I seem to be able to go inside more quickly than when I was a single woman.

Paola

One mother spoke of deciding when she had her third child that she would not get out of bed without doing meditation. "My husband really did a wonderful thing at that time. We made an arrangement where the older children would go to dad when they woke up. He would be meditating with a blanket wrapped around him and he'd open up the blanket and the children would crawl in and doze off back to sleep." Then she had her time to meditate while the baby was nursing or sleeping. She smilingly ends this tale by saying, "Is this the kind of meditation non-parents do? No. But that was what we could do."

Sometimes I would miss a day and I'd wonder if the effect was lost. But then I realized that this is a mother's life. I am not living in a Himalayan cave, just doing my practices. I learned to be flexible. If I want to do long meditation but this day, I only manage to do 5 minutes, it's okay for that day. I accept it and am happy with it.

Sevim

During the day, I could only meditate for a short time but after they went to bed, I made sure I found my own time.

Lin Hua

When my children were small, especially infants, I had to accept that my practices were not as I want, but as it comes. That is a big lesson as a mother, to give up what you would naturally do and postpone it. But then yoga became very strong for me, and I found I could do little things when they are otherwise busy, napping or whatever. I was working also but I always managed the time for yoga and meditation and in fact, I realized I needed it. Otherwise, my nerves would be driving me crazy.

Yahaira

When I first started doing yoga and meditation, I had two small children. I wanted so much to have my space that I didn't let in my youngest when I was doing my practices. He was crying in front of the door, and I didn't respond. Now I let him come in and he plays with me and sits on my lap, and it is okay. They may or may not

want to join me or do the poses with me, but I don't keep them out.
Sarala

"Mothers need to just stop. Stop everything," says a mother of four. "Make a little place where you sit with your baby or maybe the place is just for you. You've been with your baby all day and you need to have some quiet by yourself. I like paying attention to my breath, breathe in and breathe out. Or take that walk you want to take. Don't put it off."

A teacher once told me when I said that I never stopped during the day, "Just set the alarm on your phone! Set it to stop and focus, turning inwards somehow. Just set an alarm!" It was such practical advice. You have to proactively find the ways. I found every day different for me and my baby so it made it hard to trust my instincts. Making the time to stop helped me trust myself.
Sondra

To center myself, I always breathe first and foremost. The more I can stop and delight in the little things, the more I come back to myself. Every time I feed or change my baby, I try to use it as an opportunity to come back within.
Rosalyn

Breastfeeding is a mother's meditation time.
Gloriana

Many mothers agree with Gloriana that breastfeeding is a good time to go within. Because breastfeeding is such a deeply communicative act of love, using this time for meditation imprints both mother and infant with spiritual ideation. Sarkar says that for the mother to sing the Baba Nam Kevalam chant very softly while breastfeeding so that only she and her baby hear it blesses the milk and the moment.

Mothers also talk about how their children learn to accept and respect their practices. Perhaps on subconscious levels, even a small child can sense that this is something good for mama and for everyone. One mother says that when she is becoming fraught or tense, her daughter will sometimes tell her, "Mom, why don't you go do meditation?" I suspect that even babies would voice this same sentiment if they could.

> I do my practices usually before everyone wakes up but sometimes they see me in the evening. In the beginning, when they asked me what meditation was, I couldn't really explain. I used very few words which is not like me and I simply said, "It's staying in yourself." They got used to seeing me do it and now it is just a part of my life.
> Sechil

> My children understand me much better now. For example, when I'm doing yoga in the morning, my son sometimes comes in. He may climb on me or want me to play but I tell him that I need this time to be a good mommy and he usually goes out and lets me continue.
> Sarala

Both the girls would be with me many times when I meditated, sitting next to me. When I would finish and open my eyes, they were both looking at me waiting for me to stop. But they didn't usually disturb me, at least not very much.

Lin Hua

And far and away, all mothers speak of how their family benefits from their practices.

Through my meditation I have seen mistakes I made and when I do, it seems like the subconscious of the house is cleansed. The children are affected automatically.

Yvonne

I have a place where I sit to pray or meditate, and my daughters know that, and they like to be there. They understand it is a place to meditate. They go there on their own and pray in their own words. They like to look at the pictures I've put there, and they ask me many questions. We have many good talks in that meditation space.

Thekla

I realize that the children are getting something energetically from my practices. When I sit to meditate, I think it brings some clarity to the house which affects them. It became more and more clear over time that even without words, we are affecting them. I don't need to talk about

what I do or try to influence them. They get what they need to get.
Yahaira

Doing regular spiritual practice seems to create a particular kind of flow in the family. For example, the kids become so much easier that I can take care of things outside my family as well. I teach yoga and work with mothers, and they seem to understand how important that is. They don't object to my activities or to my time outside. They could make it problematic that I spend time outside the house, but they don't.
Yvonne

My children and I have a lot of conversations about spiritual things. I don't try to force them to one direction or another as I want it to be their choice. One thing is true that in our family, having a spiritual path is important. My husband is Buddhist and I follow more of a yoga path so the children will understand that there are different ways.
Themis

"There is no border between the yoga practice and life," one mother commented. "After years of practice, it gradually grows until the whole day is a yogic approach."

# Meditation & Mantras: Focusing on the Goal, Not the Obstacles

> Those who are moving will have to think constantly of their goal (Infinite Consciousness), not of their movement. If one thinks of obstacles, the obstacles themselves become one's goal, and the actual goal is relegated to the background.
>
> P.R. Sarkar, *The Macrocosmic Stance and Human Life*

Ever feel like the onslaught of difficulties brings you down more easily than the delights of life bring you up? Tantra Yoga states that the mind does indeed go down more easily than it goes up. Remarkable neuroscience research has shown that negative stimuli are perceived more easily and quickly than positive, they produce more neural activity than do equally intense positive stimuli, and they get quickly stored in long term memory circuits while positive don't. It's no wonder that at the end of the day, mom's mind remembers everything about the baby's fussiness while the infant's smile seems to slide into oblivion.

The good news is that we can strengthen the circuits for positivity. But it takes effort. In order to store a happy event for long term use, the feelings need to be consciously held in one's awareness for concentrated periods of time. Even more effective is when the remembering is accompanied by bodily feelings of happiness, viscerally and mentally making it as real as possible.

When Rafaela was weaning her third child, she knew that she would miss breastfeeding. It had always made her feel calmer and more balanced. One day, she had to attend a meeting and for some unknown reason, found herself tense, unable to concentrate. She decided to excuse herself, went into another room, sat with her eyes closed and imagined she was breastfeeding. "I could feel it so clearly and strongly, in my body, mind and heart," she relates. "It totally worked. I felt focused, calmed, and ready to go."

On a biological level, meditation has parallels to Rafaela's experience. Cellular memories created through meditation physiologically prime us to be able to recall and relive the meditative experience. A still body, focused breath and a mantra with a simple and profound meaning establish the body and mind in an inner awareness that can be called on in everyday life. Making a mantra a shelter for our thoughts deeply lodges in our cells and nerves the ideation that we are not these thoughts or actions, we are something far greater; that everything has a meaningful purpose and surrender to the Cosmic law is paramount; and that the goal of self-realization is far stronger than the passing obstacles.

Roberta, like many other meditating mothers, remembers how her mantra helped her while giving birth. "Towards the end of my first birth it was so intense that I could not even focus on drinking water, the absolute only thing I could focus on was my mantra. Unconsciously, the essence of the mantra was what gave me the ability to stay with what was happening. I think it helped me make sense of the pain and not fight it." Without pausing for a moment, she clearly expresses a truth that has become reality for her. "It's the same in life when we are given intense situations, whether physical, mental, or spiritual. The mantra brings us to levels of awareness that carry us through."

> My mantra has become my home, or the way to bring me to my own personal home. Just using it during the day is so strong for me, it helps me deal with all this other stuff.
> Romy

During labor, it was my mantra that helped me the most. I had meditated for many years before giving birth and the mantra's essence had become part of me. I just let it do the work of bringing me to where I needed to be.

Lin Hua

I use my mantra sometimes in traffic when I'm driving, and it helps me a lot. When I do it at home, I feel it cleans the air.

Yvonne

Many mothers speak of letting their children help to bring them out of a distraught mood. Playing with children, letting both the body and mind soak in their uninhibited joy works because joy is infectious. Likewise, the mantra becomes a channel for connecting with joy. And in very subtle ways, those around us feel its infectious quality.

Though Tantra Yoga meditators use a personal mantra passed on to them by trained teachers, there is a universal mantra which can be sung or listened to by anyone as a powerful meditative tool. The three Sanskrit words, Baba Nam Kevalam, roughly translate as "The essence of Love is all that exists." A more literal meaning is "Only the name of the Beloved." As mothers and infants experience love as the beloved of each other, so the same but deeper relationship exists with each of us and the Infinite Beloved. As each mother-child relationship is uniquely theirs, so the relationship of each individual with the dearest Beloved is absolutely unique and personal. Incorporating this mantra into one's life helps to imbibe the truth that this Consciousness is the most precious treasure, nearer and dearer than any other, and is not only always with us but indeed *is* who we are in our core.

The effects of this mantra may sound supremely mystical. And they are. But they are also experienced daily on a practical level. Eirini, a mother who knew this mantric chant from infant massage classes, found herself one day in the hospital's emergency room with her toddler daughter. Eirini happened upon a reference to Baba Nam Kevalam on her iPad and said it changed their whole experience.

> My daughter just had a virus infection, but we needed to wait hours to be seen. I was looking for something on my tablet to occupy her mind and came across a Facebook page about singing Baba Nam Kevalam. It could not have been a coincidence that I saw it. I started singing softly. My daughter joined me, and the time passed quickly. We didn't need any internet distractions and she became so calm that the nurses and doctors could not believe it. This chant helped us get through the ordeal so smoothly.
> Eirini

A child with too many toys becomes overwhelmed and has trouble concentrating on any of them. But give a few favorite toys, the imagination soars and the heart flies. Similarly, a mind running after everything in sight becomes exhausted and restless. A mantra-directed mind, on the other hand, thinks and acts more clearly and with more joy. The feelings of powerlessness over our runaway thoughts give way to deeper concentration, coupled with an ongoing, fascinating observation of how the mind works.

The revolutionary educator, Maria Montessori once said, "The first essential for the child's development is concentration. The child who concentrates is immensely happy." A mother's meditating mind may just be a step towards this concentrated happiness for her children and for herself.

## Recapturing Mysticism: The Soul of Meditation

> It is the embodiment of the universal spirit without which, in the 21$^{st}$ century, we as a world civilization are lost. We do not have a choice. We must rediscover the spirit of the universal mystics.
>
> Akbar S. Ahmed, *Rumi Returning*

The mystical aspect of meditative practice springs from the depth of who we are as humans. It is the boundless desire by the limited *I* for total union with the unlimited *I* - that which is love and life itself and all that gives joy. Sarkar tells us that, "Mysticism is the never-ending endeavor to merge the finite with the infinite." It is what pulls us, often unknowingly, to lose ourselves in the blissful *Self* greater than human thought or imagination. It is this mystical or devotional aspect that gives a meditative practice, or more rightly, a person's life, its juice, its heart and ultimately, its reason for existence.

> The minute I heard my first love story
> I started looking for you
> Not knowing how blind that was
> Lovers don't finally meet somewhere
> They are in each other all along
> Rumi

The human mind, in its complexity and mysteriousness, is both the hindrance and the means to the ultimate realization of the Infinite. It must be trained to experientially go beyond the intellect and emotions to the arena of unspoken oneness. The experience of this truth, gained through repeated, constant, and sincere spiritual practice, blossoms in stages. The mind gradually becomes more and more concentrated and absorbed by the mystical reality of its ideation. The Lover and the Loved become one and the same. There is no longer a hint of individuation, the small *I* has totally merged itself into Infinite Consciousness. There exists only the pin-pointed desire to be one with the Beloved as the Beloved has become all of existence, all in the created and non-created worlds. Devotion or love for the Supreme Infinite has permeated all of life.

In Tantra Yoga, this devotion is embodied in the Guru, both the physical Master and the Infinite Self residing deep within the heart. Since the nature of the human mind is to need an object, the form of Guru pulls our hearts and minds as the Beloved whom we ideate on, express ourselves to and form a relationship with.

Guru means the entity who dispels darkness. Guru and spiritual aspirant mutually attract each other. When a person thinks, "I am attracting the vast universe including Infinite Consciousness and I am also being attracted," this conscious feeling of mutual attraction is called devotion. This is much like mothers and infants. Each is magnetically attracted to the other and every loving interaction between them increases their love. If we see Guru as mother and ourselves as the children, we have begun to receive a glimpse into the dynamics of Divine Love.

> I love my child and would do anything for her to be happy. She unconditionally loves me in the same way. Realizing this made me understand more clearly than ever before what

> people mean when they talk about a
> relationship with a powerful, loving Self.
> Dora

Crucial to using this analogy well is the understanding that human relationships are limited in a way that divine relationships are not. Human relationships are between two separate entities. Although mother and infant may arguably be the closest possible that two humans can be, still they are two. But divine relationships are not between separate entities. The persona of an Infinite Entity is not a man in the sky with a long white beard who is ready to punish or reward us according to our actions but rather the deepest level of our own being. The arena of divine love happens in the farthest reaches of the heart and the secret recesses of the mind. The ensuing intimacy is one of Love with who and what we are.

The earlier in life this rhythm of love begins, the better. The mother who practices surrendering her limited *I* to the limitless *I* does herself, her child, and future generations an unparalleled service.

> Starting from early childhood one should develop the habit of self-surrender to the Supreme Entity in all thoughts and actions. There is no greater happiness or peace or joy.
> P.R. Sarkar, *Vidya Tantra and Avidya Tantra*

# Chapter 5
## Pregnant Love

*In soft whisperings from the heart the child*
*within offers you always the thread of your truth.*
Anonymous, *Celebrating Motherhood*

## The Good, the Hard, & All That's In-between

"As soon as I got the news that I was pregnant, I was bursting with self-importance and pride. I wanted to grab strangers in the supermarket and say, "Hey, I may look like a regular person but I'm pregnant, you know!" writes author Harriet Lerner about her first-time entrance into pregnancy. "The fact that other women had done this before me didn't make it feel any less like a miraculous personal achievement." This serious yet humorous account makes us smile and at the same time, may resonate deeply. It is indeed a miraculous achievement, one that has its own life force, carrying mother and baby along in its all-encompassing embrace. The ten lunar months may be anything from chaotic to peaceful, from confused uncertainty to happy excitement, or from physically sick to bursting with energy. There is no one mold and certainly no one right or best way. But whatever shows itself in a mother's body and mind, it is an unalterable game changer.

From conception on, we start to change. Like emigrants, newly pregnant mothers have

already left a familiar country and have started
a journey towards somewhere new.

Naomi Stadlen, *How Mothers Love and How Relationships
Are Born*

Pregnant mother love is an unpredictable profound journey,
potentially seasoned as much with sourness and salt as with
sweetness and honey. Physically, mother's and baby's bodies
undergo massive changes at an exponentially explosive rate.
Simultaneously, their hearts and minds are doing the same. This is
thanks, at least in part, to the increasing release of hormones, a
playing field not relegated only to the body, but which also
encompasses love and all that love entails. Mothers do not
consciously will uterine muscles to expand or blood volume to
increase or pelvic ligaments to relax, nor do they direct the mental,
emotional, or spiritual changes that are designed to happen like
clockwork in the process of becoming mothers.

Women's candid expressions of pregnant love reveal the hopes,
fears, joys, contradictions, and sense of transformation that this
time of moving into the unknown is so often about. As a first-time
mother put it, "Getting pregnant was like a bell inside me ringing
and saying, 'Look! For once in your life, look inside you.
Something is happening.' It really woke me up."

> When I first started to feel him move, I
> remember the feeling of deep connection. I
> remember the fact that I realized we heard the
> same sounds and enjoyed the same
> surroundings.
> Kinona

> Pregnancy was one of the happiest periods of
> my life, so joyful and magical though physically

it was just miserable almost from day one. I had such a strong sense that my body was not mine, as though it had become its own entity. Sometimes I felt like I, as this new entity, looked at myself saying, "Oh, you're still here!" because the whole experience was about this child, nurturing this child. I was not the same person I was before pregnancy, but I wasn't sure who I was becoming.

Karin

During my first pregnancy and up until the fifth month of gestation, life was not very easy on me. I had first of all to deal with my own emotions on whether or not I wanted to become a mother. I could count these months as the worst of my whole life as I was not comfortable with the situation. Physically I was blessed, never suffered anything that moms often mention. Emotionally I was forced in a way to go through all the phases of pregnancy and bonding. This was quite strong and after I decided to let things happen everything just seemed to fall into the right place.

Emelda

For most pregnant women, there is not a day that goes by without their thoughts being pulled inward to sense the growing baby or to reflect on their own internal changes. Along with the steady influx of needs, thoughts and feelings requiring attention, there is a deep introspective pull to pregnancy. The sense of self is undergoing a deep-rooted, moving-into-motherhood meta-morphosis. Though this inward pull may be obvious at times or nearly drowned out at other times by pressing demands, it is a real phenomenon calling women into a deeper sense of who they are.

> During my pregnancies, I felt connected to the universe in ways that I don't now that the children are so much bigger. I would look at the stars and the moon and would feel like I could be there. That feeling is not with me anymore. During pregnancies I could not tolerate anything that was violent or very harsh. I needed to be quiet, more peaceful.
> Lavanya

> During my first pregnancy, I was at ease, connected with myself and the baby, and felt very excited, happy, and feminine. The second time, it coincided with our moving house, I was very busy at work, and I had a toddler to care for. I wasn't much present with my needs nor with the baby's needs. I felt tired and stressed. Still, both times there was a deep, quiet kind of feeling, even though I was aware of it much more the first time.
> Binnur

> When pregnant with my second son, opportunities to deepen my experience with the spiritual world were always plenty and I managed to grab them. It was the most spiritual time of my life. That continued for some time after birth. It wasn't like that though with the

other two boys. But with each pregnancy, you could say I was inwardly focused.
Rhea

Pregnancy was silent, deep, and very intuitive.
Neslihan

Throughout pregnancy I wanted to do calming, peaceful activities, like walking in nature, listening to music, and meditation. Even though I had only started practicing meditation not long before becoming pregnant, it felt very natural and easy, and I really enjoyed it.
Romy

Having a baby is like the feeling of creation and God and the continuation of who you are.
Eliora

"Sometime during pregnancy, I began thinking of all the ways to describe the feelings of being pregnant," recounts Eliza, about one month after the birth of her first baby. "I was 19, this pregnancy was unplanned, I hadn't finished my schooling yet … so, as you can imagine, I had lots of conflicting feelings. But the strongest word that came to me was 'bliss.' Despite all the difficulties, this baby was, and still is, making me really happy." The minute she thought of the word "bliss," Eliza knew that this was the name she would give her son. And she did.

# Coordinated Cooperation: Partners from the Beginning

> The pregnancy with my son had its own agenda, one that ultimately meant I had to stop attempting to steer my pregnancy in the direction that I initially thought was best. I soon realized, through inner communication with my baby, that he had his own ideas of what was in his best interests, and he was a great teacher.
>
> Amali Lokugamage, *The Heart in the Womb*

A young mother named Roberta was pregnant with her first child and almost insatiably craving being in water. She so much wanted to be by the sea that she and her husband, Jason, took a trip to an island where she could swim daily. They had for some months been thinking about moving house and during this trip, sensing that their baby wanted to be near the water, they decided to move to a seaside town.

Logically speaking, relationships are two-way streets. It's clear with any two adults in a relationship that they directly affect each other. When children are born and most particularly as they grow, the extent of the mutual influence between them and their parents is undeniable. And yet, we are often blinded to this same phenomenon during pregnancy. The biological exchange of information moving from baby to mother and from mother to baby constitutes an intelligence which allows each one to adjust to the other minute by minute. This suggests a communication loop so intuitive and complex that to suppose it only affects physical changes is missing crucial parts of the whole picture. We have well documented in recent decades that the mother's thoughts and feelings directly influence the mind of the infant, before as much as after birth. What about the other way around? Might the unborn infant's mind be affecting the mother just as much, although in a subtler way? What might the infant be conveying?

In Eleni's first pregnancy, she recalls that she was very quiet and wanted to be alone a lot. Her son before birth was quiet and still is. "The lessons he offers are through silence," she says. "During pregnancy, we had a communication, and it was complete, even better than the communication I have with most adults. Most of the time, it had to do with reassurance and relaxation – not at all weird if you think I was so stressed during that period." Her second pregnancy was much different. She felt more like her usual self but even more than usual. "I was very extroverted, loud, expressive, without caring much about what other people have to say. My second child is just like this, loud, expressive, loves to sing and dance, and always comes forward to do anything for anyone she loves."

> With my second pregnancy, I went through ups and downs, but nothing really got me down. Usually, I am a stressed person, but I felt the support of this baby during pregnancy, and nothing could shake me. I was so happy; it was just too good to let any shadows pass over it. Even as an infant, he still has a soothing effect on me.
> Arianna

> I was very calm during pregnancy even though the surroundings around me were falling to bits. I think that was the influence of the baby.
> Maryam

During one of my pregnancies, I was in a very, very stressful and difficult situation. And at one point I was so upset that I thought I might miscarry. When I look back now, I think that the baby carried me through that time. She was like a protector, and she still is.

Lavanya

During my first pregnancy, I was so sure I was having a girl that I was very surprised when he came out a boy. I seemed somehow attached to the thought of a girl and didn't let it go. He is a very willful, clear, and strong-minded child, holding onto thoughts like I was in his pregnancy. His brother is a lot more adaptable and flowing and that's how I was in his pregnancy.

Ramona

Might the infant be communicating concrete needs and desires? "The new life inside the pregnant woman takes over in order to prepare the mother to provide for this unique child in ways that the mother does not yet understand," observes a mother of three. "These are the first lessons for us. These realizations, which are the voice of the unborn child, are our first training in learning to trust that the child knows what he needs, understands who we are, and is able to communicate."

Arianna tells of her son being breech a week before birth. Though she was concerned about this, she was trying to accomplish many things before the birth and wasn't slowing down to get ready. Finally, she understood that by being breech he was saying, "Well, if you are rushing around everywhere and not getting ready, I will sit right up until you notice me." When she said, "Ok, ok let's do it," he turned head down. She goes on to say that she felt like they were one mind, a sentiment echoed by other mothers.

> In the second trimester of pregnancy, we traveled to Mexico and Arizona to special spiritual places. I am sure my son-in-utero was the one who took us there. He wanted to go to those places. We went to a Sundance with some native American friends and now he stops and listens intently when he hears drums, like those at the Sundance.
> Diana

> I am positive that my unborn daughter drove me to choose a homebirth. At first, I was planning to go to the hospital in the very usual, standard way. But then, the idea of homebirth kept coming to us in different ways. Finally, in the sixth month, friends talked about their homebirth and after that, I knew but I resisted. I could not sleep for three days from utter fear coming from the conviction that birthing at home was the "truth" for me. And of course, it was. I am sure she had something to do with that.
> Eleanora

Besides communicating his own needs, the prenate may be communicating an understanding of the mother's needs and how they fit together with his.

> Towards the end of pregnancy, I started having doubts, wondering if I could be a good mother. One day I sat down and spontaneously began

writing about all the things that had led up to
me being a mother. I felt that all these thoughts,
or the impetus to do it, was coming through the
baby. I think she gave me that insight. The next
day I went into labor.
Noriah


My son led me into yoga. I had done some
before being pregnant with him but not a lot
and never consistently. Quite near the
beginning of his pregnancy, I wanted to do yoga
and went to a pregnancy yoga class. Right away
I felt like I was home and now, several years
later, I am a qualified yoga teacher, and it has
become a big part of my everyday life. He is
still small but even now, he likes to join me.
Sevim


Sometimes mothers have dreams, cravings, or behavior
patterns they never had before and often never have again. Perhaps
some or all of these are communication from the unborn baby.
Ayurvedic doctor Robert Svoboda writes that, "Most of these
desires (cravings) reflect the preferences and aversions of the fetus
which are carried over from previous existences and transmitted to
the mother through the channels that connect them influencing
her feelings and perceptions."


My daughter was born very allergic. Before I
was pregnant, I was vegetarian but when I got
pregnant, I was craving meat. I ate a lot of meat.
I couldn't eat fish though I love fish. She is
allergic to fish, but she loves meat. With my
son, I didn't want to eat meat much, but I

wanted to eat fish a lot. He likes fish much more than meat. I wanted to eat a lot of lemons and he loves lemons.
Sechil

I became very sensitive to noise; noise stressed me during pregnancy. My son is noise-sensitive and I'm thinking it is because of him that I became so sensitive. Also, there was no way I could sit on a chair after finishing lunch or dinner which is a habit he still has. I started to eat okra during my pregnancy. I had never eaten it before, nor after, but my son loves it. I remember a craving for peanut butter which was very bizarre since it is something I don't usually like. He loves peanut butter. I listened a lot to classical music but was especially drawn to Schubert, something not usual for me. He loves Schubert.
Carolina

In my first pregnancy, I wanted to eat a lot of hot spicy foods which is not like me usually. My daughter likes hot spicy foods.
Miki

It is most probably true, however, that some cravings come primarily from the nutritional needs of the mother and not from the infant.

When I was pregnant with my daughter, I was eating buckets of apples, but she has no particular like or dislike for them. During the

pregnancy of one of my sons I was eating a lot
of lemons. Kilos of lemons every day! The boy
hates lemons, he had enough in my tummy.
Vandana

While certainly the give-and-take is a mutual exchange, there
may be no clear-cut conclusions to the questions of mother-infant
influence. As one mother said, "I am not sure if these behaviors
(during pregnancy) were mine, affecting the babies or derived
from the babies and I was just acting as their mirror." And, in fact,
it may not even be necessary or possible to know definitively. The
crux of the matter is that, without a doubt, the exchange between
mother and unborn infant is deep, strong and mutual.

Let's look again at Roberta and Jason, the parents whose story
started this section. They moved to the sea because they
instinctively felt that their son wanted that, and they never
regretted their decision. Their example is about acknowledging gut
feelings that come from an intricate web of needs which includes
the unborn baby in the dialogue. The conversation for most
people may not be as concretely about issues like where to live but
rather reflects bigger consciousness changes. As Roberta and Jason
moved from non-parents to parents, in the process of discovering
what it's all about they took into consideration what the child
seemed to be saying. Doing that created for them a sense of family
dynamics inclusive of and respectful to all its members.

Children, even unborn ones, may be showing us truths unknown
to us and one of our main jobs may be to fine tune our listening.


## The Two-in-One Phenomenon

It is a common relationship between mothers
and babies where the mother, at least, feels the

baby to be an extension of herself ... in a sphere of intimacy whose boundary defines their common identity. Psychologists tell us the baby feels the same.

Danah Zohar, *The Quantum Self*

Pregnancy is perhaps literally and metaphorically the closest two human beings can be. Physically, there is no other naturally occurring example of one person living within another. This two-in-one phenomenon is described by Sandra Steingraber in *Having Faith: An Ecologist's Journey to Motherhood* as an intertwining of mother and child in the closest kind of embrace biologically possible. Ayurvedic practitioner Robert Svoboda describes it as a two-hearted psychological unit. Heart-to-heart, body-to-body, mind-to-mind, and soul-to-soul, pregnancy begins a profound, lifelong partnership. Rudolf Steiner, philosopher and founder of Anthroposophy, asserts that psychic umbilical cords form during pregnancy along with the physical cord. Though the physical cord is cut at birth, the psychic cords exist always, connecting mother and child in a very real mutual influence even if they are separated by great distances.

In my first pregnancy, and from the very first months, I had the strong and constant feeling that I have a friend along with me. Wherever I was going, I was never alone. This feeling was comforting and reassuring. This sense of being together as one stayed with me until the end. I was telling the baby that we are two bodies in the same one, and that we will separate just for a little and then be together again as long as we live. And I don't know where these thoughts were coming from.

Aniisha

During pregnancy, I had the strangest feeling that my daughter and I were one being, just in two different bodies. When I gave birth, I didn't feel like we became separate entities, it still felt like we were one. Even now, she's almost three years old and when I look at her it's hard for me to understand that she is someone separate from me. It's a unique dynamic. There is a really strong psychic umbilical cord between us.

Anat

Perhaps the multitude of changes during pregnancy are truly meant to stir deeper thoughts of who we are. Tantra Yoga speaks of all of life as existing within the mind of an Absolute Primordial Consciousness, two-in-one (or many in one) played out on a cosmic scale. We live within the womb of the Great Mother or the mind of the Great Father or the soul of the Ultimately Great Love. As the infant cannot exist without the mother during pregnancy and will always be connected to her on very deep levels, so we do not ever exist separately from the Consciousness of Life. As children are made up of DNA inherited from their parents, so we are made of Consciousness itself, shaped into billions of different forms. Children turn to mother for solace, care, and guidance and in the same way, we turn inward to our deepest intuitive self. Mother-child love is deeply rewarding and motivating to both partners and the same is true of a greater Love. Our hearts are warmed by this Love while Love Itself is enriched and, put metaphorically in human terms, very happy to have us in Its embrace.

Consciousness cannot, of course, truly be defined in human terms and yet, the human mind relishes a frame of reference with which it is familiar to understand abstract concepts of great magnitude. Hence, a Tantra Yoga term such as Infinite Consciousness or Love or the Greater Self, embodied and exemplified by the guru or spiritual master, could just as rightly be called God or any other term that resonates. What it's about in the end is the personal relational aspect of the Divinity within each of us. It is this that the mother-infant relationship has the extraordinary potential to pull us towards.

## Asking the Big Questions

Pariprashna (in Sanskrit) means those questions which are responsible for our spiritual elevation. It means to know what to do and how to do it. Pariprashna has ... only one import, and that is that you are to ask a question in order to get a certain reply and that reply will be followed by you in the practical field.

P.R. Sarkar, *The Three Factors for Spiritual Elevation*

An astounding physiological adaptation that reflects the profound changes in a mother's consciousness lies in the brain itself. To fulfill the tasks mother love requires, women's brains undergo very observable changes, one being a decrease in size during pregnancy. Beginning around six months of pregnancy, writes Louann Brizendine in *The Female Brain*, women's brains begin to shrink. But we are not losing brain cells. On the contrary, synaptic connections are massively reorganizing themselves, strengthening the pathways most necessary for mothering, letting the less necessary dwindle away and all the while creating entirely new ones. When new mothers say they feel that they are redefining themselves, it is truly their neurons speaking. The empty-headed forgetfulness many pregnant women experience in the second and third trimesters and just after birth may be due to this massive reorganization of priorities. Beginning to enlarge around one to two weeks before birth, the coming online of a newly enriched brain allows new mothers to be more perceptive, efficient, resilient, motivated, altruistic, and what many see as emotionally and oftentimes, spiritually intelligent. By around six months after birth when the brain has again reached its normal size, mothers are more equipped and ready for the lifelong journey they have embarked on.

While the brain is making space for new and deeper ways of looking at life, pregnant mothers may ask questions like, "Who and what is this growing life within me? What is the source of this life? What is pregnancy showing me?"

> It's a miracle. I don't know what else to say. Looking at my child and saying who are you? Where did you come from? They are such spiritual beings in front of my eyes and make me think about deeper things. To see your own child grow and change makes you know there is more than just biology in this. I wasn't brought up believing in God or any particular religion, so I have enjoyed this spiritual journey through my children.
>
> Sondra

"The human brain appears to be organized to ask meaningful questions and seek meaningful answers," reports the Commission for Children at Risk. Tantra Yoga sees questioning as a natural and necessary tool in the perennial human need to understand and absorb life. It is during times of the greatest upheavals in life that sincere questioning leads to insights into personal or social transformation. "We can only know the aspect of reality we are looking for," says quantum physicist Danah Zohar. "Our answers will always be answers only to the questions we ask."

A mother asking these questions will be conveying to her baby that such questions are important. Since the big questions in life need to be asked again and again, over years and lifetimes, meditative spiritual practices can be an invaluable construct within which realizations may surface. But Pariprashna does not mean endless questioning from mere curiosity. It implies a sincere desire to gain understanding into the mysteries of life and being ready to act on them, regardless of the obstacles or resistance they may bring.

Rather than trying to give our children the answers to life, our contribution might more aptly be to model for them asking the right questions, listening for the responses, and letting those responses guide our way.

## Chapter 6
# Birth Love

*Of the sadness or joy, good fortune or tragedy that awaits every mother and newborn in this life we can never know in advance. But the birth journey is and will always be nothing short of heroic for every child and every mother, every time.*

Kemp Battle, *Celebrating Motherhood*

## Being Born & Giving Birth: Tantric Struggle & Surrender

I remember visiting a woman named Sandy the day after the homebirth of her first child. When I enter her house, I find her sitting in a very comfortable looking rocking chair in front of a warm winter fire with her one-day old infant at her breast. She looks at me with the timeless eyes of a woman who has just been to the center of existence and back, full of awe, disbelief, and a deeply quiet serenity. "What happened here yesterday was not of my doing." The words slide out of her as though coming from an unseen and previously unknown part of her being. "I am not a religious person, but I have to say that what we went through in the birth was so much bigger than life, bigger than any life I have ever known. And something *big* not only orchestrated it but literally carried us through it."

Her impassioned voice reflects the freshness of her birth memories as she recalls how the beginning of labor had not been too hard but as it intensified, she reached a point where she thought she could no longer do it. "I was starting to feel desperate, on the verge of panic. And then something astounding happened. I let go, or gave in, or gave over – I simply surrendered. I just knew that I had to ride with what was happening and not try to control it. When I totally let go and sank into the experience, the baby came quickly."

What Sandy was surrendering to was the power of life itself. The physical act of birthing is beyond the control of mother or doctor or baby or anyone else present. It happens through an intelligence which many refer to as the intelligence of the body, but which could more aptly be called the Infinite Intelligence of all that is. Opening to that pulls both mother and baby into what Michel Odent has called "an expanded awareness in the process of a joyous birth." It is the self meeting the Self. The limited *I* giving over to the limitless *I*.

Birth is a profound act of creativity. Creativity is a process, not a finished product. Surrendering our hopes, desires, fears, and expectations is perhaps one of the greatest and most rewarding challenges of being human. "With every contraction," remembers a mother named Eleanora about her second labor, "I said 'Yes.' I welcomed each one, said, 'Yes' when it came and by the end of labor, I found myself saying, 'Thank you' when the contraction finished. 'Yes,' focus, 'Thank-you,' pause. That was the rhythm. I was never fighting it because I knew if I went with it, I would open up."

> It was so intense and beyond anything my body had ever experienced. Added to that was an anxiousness I felt because my midwife hadn't arrived. When she came, I told her, "This hurts so bad." She immediately stopped me by

replying, "Don't go there in your mind." It was exactly what I needed to hear. She told me to go within and when I did, it wasn't a painful sensation anymore. It was a force, a primal force surging through me.

Noriah

The mother's state of mind depends on how much you surrender. Once you let it take you, you're in another reality. It's a very strong experience in your body and at the same time, out of it, happening on different levels.

Regina

Let's stop for a minute to look at surrender in light of what many people assume it to be. It is often misinterpreted as being either passive or defeatist. We are people who like to be in control of our lives and surrender seems to negate that. "Most people have negative associations to the very word," writes Harriet Lerner in *Mother Dance.* "To surrender is to lose, to throw our hands up in the air, to admit defeat. Surrender has connotations of giving up or failing rather than giving ourselves over to forces or events larger than we are."

By its very nature, birth has the potential to reverse the negative idea of surrender. Many mothers come through birth with a very deep appreciation for the sacredness and practical value of surrender in their everyday lives. When life seems bigger or harder than we can bear, our awareness needs to expand to take in the big picture. This is not giving up. Rather, it is stepping back into an objective self who is watching the scenario while simultaneously, the subjective self is living it. This has the potential to bring clarity and reaffirm purpose.

The whole labor, especially as it became more intense, seems now, looking back at it, like such a contradiction. I was totally in the awareness of the contractions and their unbelievable intensity and at the same time, I was watching them come and go, observing them rise and peak and fall. It was being aware of several levels of existence at once.

Ilaira

The thought that naturally pops up is, "If such surrender and resultant bliss works during labor, why wouldn't it work in the myriad of other small and large 'births' in our everyday lives?" Throughout life, we never stop "birthing" new ideas, relationships, or activities. Many of our greatest accomplishments are born after periods of gestation and through intense effort. In fact, being driven to desperation can at times be the exact impetus needed to initiate a major breakthrough in life.

The truth is that how we are born and how we give birth are critical foundational experiences for how we meet challenges throughout life. A point to remember is that we are never alone in our challenges. The mother is not giving birth alone. Nor is the infant being born alone. They are birthing together. And the mother-infant dyad is not doing it alone. They are doing it with the support of the greatest power in existence. The kind of message that we would like to see embodied in all infants entering this life and all mothers entering into motherhood goes something like this: "Life is full of challenges, some of them long, extreme, and painful. But we can do it. We can step into whatever life brings with the knowledge that love and support is there for us. We are not alone. We have the internal resources to meet any challenge, big or small. The deepest truth is that Infinite Love, our constant source of strength, is our own inner self."

It's like reaching the top of the mountain, the feeling after having given birth. It feels like, "If I can do this, I can do anything." It has humbled me every time and also made me more courageous.

Karin

I remember moments of desperation during my first labor when the urge to give up was enormous. Had I been in the hospital at that point, I would surely have asked for pain medication. But I'm grateful that I couldn't. Going through those moments has helped me many times in my mothering life. When mothering seems too great a task and I feel I've reached my limit, I have to move out of my head and into my center, like I was during labor and after the baby was born. Then I know full well that I can do what needs to be done.

Raquel

The dynamic biological link between mother and child during labor and birth is based on love. The hormones which stimulate uterine contractions are also hormones of love. These, together with a mix of other naturally occurring chemical substances released during birth, do not take away the intensity of labor but rather act as an undercurrent of stamina and endurance. Though that love may not be sensed by conscious layers of the mind, its presence is a powerful stabilizing force for both mother and infant. It pulls the mother's mind inward towards a spacious but focused awareness and unconsciously keeps her going when she might otherwise give up. The same is most probably true for the baby.

In our everyday lives, the inherent bond of love between our individual sense of *I* and our expanded sense of Infinite *I* does not take away the challenges or difficulties, nor does it shield us from pain. But, as in childbirth, it is the deep stabilizing force helping us find balance and joy and keeping us on track.

> Giving birth really connected to me to a deep sense of myself and life; you can call it spiritual. This has always stayed with me.
> Ira

> I think I only withstood the labor pains because of some deep feeling of not being alone but being protected and guided. The only way I can describe it is like something angelic holding me and taking care of me even though the physical pain was so intense I thought I wouldn't make it.
> Aniisha

At the core of Tantra Yoga teachings is the saying, "Struggle is the essence of life." Though at first glance, this may seem pessimistic, it is, in fact, quite the opposite. Profound change always comes from what Sarkar calls clash and cohesion. Intense clashes push, pull, twist, and turn us until we have seen ways of being that are deeper and more meaningful than we had previously known. And in the seeing of a bigger picture, we experience the joy of developing a more cohesively integrated mind, physically, mentally, and spiritually.

> The unit mind finds natural problems which it must solve, such as procuring food, finding accommodation, and rearing children — not to mention simply staying alive. The more

difficult these obstacles are, the more scope the mind gets to unfold. The struggle to overcome obstacles is the primary factor in the development of the mind.

P.R. Sarkar, *Sadhana*

Tantra Yoga says that while life is a continuous rhythm of obstacles pushing us to our limits and beyond, we are never faced with difficulties greater than our capacity to overcome. Furthermore, each obstacle or challenge is an ally in our move towards realization of the Great, each one a friend to be welcomed for the strength, resilience, and understanding it bestows. And even further still is the teaching that says, "The nobler the task, the mightier the obstacles." As daunting as that may sound, it is indeed a truth that nearly any mother who has given birth can testify to.

Giving birth was certainly the hardest thing I've ever done in my life and just as certainly the most rewarding.

Renee

I remember reading long ago that in ancient Aztec culture, after a baby was born, the tribe honored the mother in a way similar to the celebration of a man returning victorious from war. It was recognized how extraordinary is the strength of mind and stamina of spirit needed in both instances.

I realized that we as women and mothers are very powerful warriors. As a child I thought women exaggerated when they talked about giving birth but now, I know they were right.

Lilith

Zoe's birth with her third child exemplifies this kind of Tantric spirit. She showed acceptance and surrender at the same time as determinedly pursuing what she knew was right. Her first two children were born by cesarean. Years later, when she found herself unexpectedly pregnant again, she searched for but could not find any doctor or midwife in her area who would do a VBAC (Vaginal Birth After Cesarean). But she decided that this birth would be different. "If I was going to give birth by cesarean, I would try to do a natural cesarean. I did a lot of research and came up with many steps that I presented to the doctor." These steps included keeping the lights in the surgical room low, playing music that she liked, having the baby immediately on her chest, not cutting the cord until it stopped pulsing, not suctioning the baby but rather squeezing his chest as he was born as would have happened coming through the birth canal, and having an independent midwife with her to make sure these requests would be honored. These ideas were extremely radical at the time; her doctor had never heard of any of them, and he strongly resisted. But she would not back down. It took a lot to persuade him. In the end, he did agree to most of the steps.

Having done all this preparation, Zoe was able to be in the experience with a quiet, centered mind. She went into labor at four in the morning and her son was eventually born by cesarean at 6 p.m. "I knew that by that time, he was ready to come out," she remembers. During the surgery, a song was playing that she and her baby had listened to all through pregnancy. She lovingly found herself telling her infant, "You know you're going to be born, this is our song." He was placed immediately on her chest, and they were not separated except when his father held him. "Even though there were still a few medical steps that I would have liked to forgo, it all felt good. I think my son was aware of our intentions and that's what was important." Zoe ended her story with the thought, "It's worth fighting harder for the important things in life."

The challenges that truly stretch us often bring us to the point of desperation, of feeling that the task is too big and that we are not capable. It is not uncommon for women in labor to reach this point. Sometimes consciously but oftentimes not, this may translate into a feeling of being confronted with death. Looking death in the eyes can be a singularly empowering experience. Death in its broadest sense is the transformation of an entity into something new. A person dies and leaves the body but is subsequently reborn into another body, a new form. We struggle with a thought or a question and finally, understanding comes in the form of a new thought or even a new question. When the ego, or the limited *I* dies, it gains expanded new life as it merges into the Infinite *I*. "At a certain point of labor, the woman has the feeling that I am going to die," says the long-time birth activist, Frederick Leboyer. "And she accepts in order to save the child. What dies is not her body. It is the little ego that vanishes and the moment that happens, she becomes boundless, limitless just like life."

> In transition, I looked at my midwife and asked her, "Am I going to die?" and she said, "Yes, the old you is dying to the new you."
> Eleftheria

> In my first birth, I faced death. My body felt like it was going to explode. Those kinds of sensations were so unfamiliar and so strange that at a certain point, I thought I might have stopped existing. I really wondered if I was dead or alive. Where is my body, where am I, what happened to me? Then I heard my midwife's voice and I thought, "Did she also die and come

with me?" I laugh about it now but at the time, it was all very real.

Aniisha

"You feel like you're going to die but not because of the body," one mother said, "but because the mind is in a state of touching its limits. It's as if there is a door open a bit in front of you and death is on the other side and you can't do anything about it." At some point, she realized she had no choice but to surrender, and the baby came soon after.

Tantra Yoga says that all human egos, all egoistic expressions, are based on the vanity moving around the self, moving around the *I* feeling. I think, I do, I have ... all these *I*'s are ultimately surrendered through repeatedly directing one's mind towards the source of all life. This is done within oneself in a meditative form called dhyana in which the limited *I* realizes itself as Pure Consciousness. It is also done by recognizing Consciousness in all forms of existence. Everything is Consciousness — me, you, others, things, feelings, ideas and everything in the created world.

A useful Tantra Yoga teaching to remember is that if we have potentialities that we are not using because we need to learn about surrender, circumstances will be created in which the ego will be forced to yield. Actions occur ranging from mildly embarrassing to humiliatingly humbling. This is certainly true for all of us many times in our lives. In other words, we are forced to acknowledge the Infinite Self behind our ability to think and act. It is in this surrender that Sarkar says, "Your soul will have its full expression."

# The Birthing Mind: Maintaining Inner Focus

Close the language door and open the love window.
Rumi

Describing the advent of life on this planet, P.R. Sarkar tells us that for life to have come into being and continue to exist, two conditions were necessary. The first is that, of the opposing forces inherent in atoms and all of life, the interior, *center-seeking force must be stronger than the exterior pulling force.* This maintains the nucleus or core of the structure. The second requirement is that *the environment must be right.* Birthing a new life into existence is as dependent on these elements as was the birth of the first life forms millions of years ago.

Let's look at the first requirement, *a strong center-seeking force.* There is a thread of commonality running through the experiences of unimpeded, intuitive births and that is slipping into a non-ordinary state of mind, a 'birthing mind' so to speak. When the mother-infant mind is dominated by an outward or centrifugal force, it becomes stuck in cortical, linear thinking focused on fears, doubts, and the attempt to control the process. But when the center seeking or centripetal force is stronger, awareness is pulled away from thinking into experiencing and thus is able to transcend into subtler levels.

> I wasn't thinking about my breathing or the people around me, though I was aware of it all. When I felt the contraction coming on, I'd feel my mind getting really focused and then I felt like my mind was going into it. I was sinking into the experience of it. That's the only way I can describe it. I didn't fight it; I just went with it.
> Carole

Some women will naturally fall into such a centered place during labor. "It just happened naturally," Carole remembers. "I didn't do anything, really, it just went on its own."

> Before I gave birth, I read a book talking about how in natural childbirth women go to an altered state of consciousness and I didn't like that. I like to know what's going on. I like to be in control and so that frightened me. But when the time came for me to give birth it felt very natural. You don't disconnect at all. In fact, if anything you're more connected. It's bizarre. You're totally in your body. I remember holding my baby afterwards thinking, "I did this without any fear." There's pain, there's struggle and all of that but there's no fear, there's complete trust. It's a very positive altered state.
> Anat

Having done meditation before birth, or some kind of practice which requires both concentration and surrender, can be of tremendous help to a mother. She may be able to use her meditation rhythm during birth or, in her own way, go through labor with an inner equanimity. Tantra Yoga practices include training in withdrawing the awareness from outside stimuli and internal thoughts, directing the mind to a certain focal point, and letting the resultant shift in consciousness occur.

> Years of meditation gave me some tools for labor. Using the mantra was really helpful in maintaining a focus. Meditation builds up willpower and stamina at sitting and focusing for a long time. That's the thing about labor,

you need the focus and concentration and the capacity to stick with it. I think meditating beforehand helped me with that.
Ramona

I had gone to classes where they told us about breathing and so on, but I didn't find that so helpful. My meditation practice is what helped me more.
Lin Hua

I definitely think that meditation was a big factor in being able to have the birth experience that I had. Meditation prepared my mind. It was familiar ground. My mind knew what it felt like to be focused. When these neural pathways are burned into your mind, they are familiar, and your mind is more likely to go there. It helped my sense of concentration.
Kendra

I felt like there was very little going on in my head during the whole experience, very little mind chatter. I was present and here in the moment. There is a similar experience that happens in meditation when the mind chatter quiets down and you open into other states of being.
Carmen

Beginning a meditation practice can even happen during pregnancy. Zeynep enrolled in a yoga course in mid-pregnancy and loved the meditation part at the end of class. She found it so useful and soothing that she managed at least several times a week to sit in silence, focus on her breath and let the Baba Nam Kevalam yogic chant envelop her mind. "I am quite sure it helped me in labor," she remembers. "I kept hearing the chanting in my mind. It changed melody several times, just on its own, but it seemed to keep me going."

But not all women fall into a focused birthing mind so easily. "If only I'd known what I know now," Zoe says, especially in relation to her first birth. "I felt like I gave away my power to the nurses, the midwives, the doctors, and the medical system."

> I think most people haven't had an experience of deep meditation and of feeling their central core of power. If I'd had that experience in my life before I labored with my son, if I could have drawn on that deep powerful center in myself, I'm sure that would have helped me, and things could have turned out differently. But I didn't know that then.
>
> Zoe

Her son ended up being born by cesarean and that set the precedent for her remaining two births to also be cesarean. But by the time of her third birth, she was much wiser. Though she was having surgery, she managed to keep her mind in a very deep and quiet center.

> Almost instinctively, intuitively, I went into that deep, quiet center in myself. The whole thing was calm, and I felt very protected. I think in labor if you can go there, that's the place that channels the universal life stream. I have a deep sense that there's a truth there. I suppose its defining quality is that it's utterly still and it

> connects with everything around me. In labor,
> if you can get past the fear of what your body is
> doing, then it can be so beautiful. Then there is
> no good or bad. That's the essence of it.
> Zoe

As Zoe's story makes clear, the beauty of the birthing mind is that it does not need to have a specific setting or a pre-ordained birth outcome. It is connecting with a deeper *I* which is not dependent on time, place, or person. It is about maintaining an expanded awareness, a connection to Consciousness. And those are purely inner qualities.

Arcana's birth with her first child is an example of how a mother can stay in her heart and maintain this connection even in unpredictable circumstances. Her plan was to give birth at home but as life has it, complications arose and Arcana found herself in the hospital, being prepped for a cesarean. She was determined that her son's birth would be a good one, no matter what the external situation. As she was lying on the operating table with the obstetrician beginning the surgery, she started to sing a yoga chant called the Gayatri Mantra. She didn't ask anyone if she could sing or care what anyone thought, she just sang to her baby from her heart. Much to her surprise, a few minutes later, the doctor started singing. He wasn't singing the Gayatri Mantra, but a song that he knew and liked. Moments later, the nurse began singing and then the anesthesiologist until finally, everyone in the operating room had burst out in song. Each person singing something different could have been a disastrous cacophony of sound, but it wasn't. Arcana said it was beautiful. As her son was placed on her chest, she felt him to be peaceful. He had emerged into a symphony of music that transformed the moment into what she had hoped for.

# The Birthing Mind: Maintaining Outer Balance

> Be with those who help your being. Don't sit
> with indifferent people whose breath comes
> cold out of their mouths. Your work is deeper.
> Rumi

The second component in the formation of life, *the environment must be right*, is equally as important as the mother's or couple's personal readiness. The birth environment means the people whom the mother has chosen to have with her and the setting she places herself in.

Many birthing couples believe that safety means being with highly trained medical professionals who are able to perform emergency care in the best equipped clinical setting. This may be true, and gratefully so, for pregnancies at risk but when applied to all births, it perpetuates the fearful idea that birth is inherently dangerous. The desired outcome in this scenario is a "healthy" baby and mother, meaning that the infant's body is intact and functioning properly and the mother has no serious physical complications. Birth, however, is about much more than emergency care and bodies in one piece. The essential elements on which the physical rests are those of the mind, heart, and soul.

"But what if something goes wrong?" The fear of birth naturally brings up this thought in loving and concerned parents. In a normally healthy mother and normally healthy baby, going right rather than wrong is the inherent design. A midwife friend once wisely said, "Pregnant women are the only people routinely checked into a hospital when something is *right* with them, not when something is wrong."

Powerful and negative media images greatly influence current perceptions of childbirth. Too many media scenarios are of laboring women screaming in pain, begging for help or medication, rushing panic-stricken to the hospital, calling out for the doctor and so on. It's very hard for images such as these to not affect women and men alike. A calm, uncomplicated birth where the mother is doing well in labor is far less often depicted in the media. Combine that with stories of terrible birth experiences handed down sometimes from generation to generation and it's no wonder we feel afraid.

Women innately know how to give birth though we may have forgotten and need support to remember. And infants innately know how to be born. Women who feel incompetent, observed, fearful, or helpless are more likely to experience greater pain and more complications in labor than women who feel supported, capable, respected, and able to follow her instincts. Those who will attend the birth — midwives, doctors, doulas, fathers, partners, friends, or relatives — and the place of birth need to be carefully and soul-searchingly selected with resonance only the heart can understand.

## Birth Attendants

> You are a birth servant. Do good without show or fuss. If you must take the lead, lead so that the mother is helped, yet still free and in charge. When the baby is born, they will rightly say, 'We did it ourselves!'
> *Tao Te Ching*

"For my first child, I had a wonderful midwife with me," recalls Sondra. "I felt safe. The most important thing was trust. I just trusted that this was right, and it was going to happen, and I could do it. I never felt helpless. I think a lot of it was having the right people with me."

Mothers are the ones giving birth, babies are the ones being born, and those who are invited are the ones supporting them. I remember reading once that instead of talking about "delivering" a baby, the thinking of a particular traditional culture was that the midwives 'received' the baby. For birth attendants, it is a privilege to receive babies into this world.

This thinking may require a stretch in perspectives, both for the parents and the birthing team alike. Mothers are too often disempowered, feeling inadequate for the task at hand and medical people are too often overly empowered, seeing themselves as needing to step up to the plate and be in charge.

> I recently read about how natural birth can be and I felt, "Oh, my God! I totally didn't do it that way!" I had two elective cesareans because I got afraid and let the doctors do everything. If I would have had people around me who were aware of natural birth and if I'd trusted those people, it might have been different.
> Sevim

The norm in many places is for mothers to give birth under the care of an obstetrician. Obstetricians, however, are generally trained in what can go wrong, when and how to intervene, and the use of medicine, medical equipment, and surgery. The average obstetricians may truly be caring and well-intentioned but will naturally practice in the way they have been taught. According to the late physician and birth advocate, Marsden Wagner, "Having a highly trained obstetrical surgeon attend a normal birth is analogous to having a pediatric surgeon babysit a healthy two-year-old." I often compare it to bringing in a bulldozer to clear away a few small stones.

While there certainly are exceptionally sensitive and attuned obstetricians, it is generally the midwifery/doula model of care that adapts itself to normally healthy women and infants at birth. Women with women is a traditional model of birthing which has been lost in many countries. Midwives and doulas may fill this gap by supporting the mother rather than projecting the medical model of managing the birth. "When authentic midwifery is rediscovered," wrote the obstetrician and birth activist Michel Odent, "obstetricians can recover their genuine role as experts in unusual and pathological situations."

> I was in such pain and trying to be strong and not react because I didn't want my midwife to think that I needed a cesarean. Finally, I gave in and told the midwife how much it hurt. She looked at me, gave me a kiss on the top of my head and said, "I know it does." That was all I needed. I went from 3 cm to fully dilated in no time and then birthed easily.
> Demetra

> The midwife and my husband were great, but it was my doula who really helped me during labor. She somehow knew exactly where to push on my back to relieve the pressure, she seemed to know when I needed a hug and when I wanted to be left alone. I was so grateful she was there.
> Renee

> My midwife trusted me and didn't interfere during labor. I was aware of others but felt like I was in a cave with other women. I had a surge

of a very, very ancient feeling. I didn't want to be touched. I knew everything was fine.

Hannah

I was trying to block the pain and finally I couldn't and started letting out very loud, long sounds. I am not the type to be loud at all, I am very quiet but once I let myself be loud, I just kept going. The nurses came rushing in saying I needed an epidural, but my midwife understood that I didn't, that I was just expressing. And she was right. If she hadn't been there to protect me, I don't think I could have stayed focused and dealt with the nurses at the same time.

Dorothea

This is not, however, a story of good guys and bad guys. It's a story of people on both sides of the divide — parents and birth attendants alike — trapped in the web of birthing systems needing a major overhaul. The important point is the heart and mind of the practitioner rather than her or his training or job title. It is an attitude of trust and respect combined with knowledge of the birth process that birthing women and infants need.

## The Place of Birth

For me, home was very safe and probably safer than the hospital. I was more relaxed at home. But if a woman doesn't feel like that or is overwhelmed, she needs to give birth where she feels safest.

Kiirana

The best place for a woman to give birth is where she is most comfortable. Sometimes women feel pressured to give birth someplace when they would rather be somewhere else. The most common is pressure to go to the hospital when an out-of-hospital setting feels better. On the other hand, a woman can feel pressure to have a home birth when her friends are doing that but in her heart, she doesn't feel safe at home.

"All mammals on earth seek out the quietest, safest, most private dark spot when they get ready to deliver," says human development researcher, Joseph Chilton Pearce, in the video series *Reaching Beyond Magical Child.* "And we act out of that mammalian brain. Any mammal on earth receives the signal to stop the birth process if that safe, secure, dark hideaway is interrupted. Any interference in the birth process will cause any mammal to stop and wait for the coast to be clear or the danger to be removed. The mother may even change her birthing place. This is inherent in our whole system."

The birth room must be serene. There should be no one who is afraid since in such a setting, fear is palpable and spreads easily. There ought not to be unnecessary conversation or intrusive observation. The mother must move about as necessary, be uninhibited to vocalize as she feels, have respectful support around her and let her consciousness shift from normal mind into birthing mind.

> I was making a lot of noise though I wasn't really that conscious of it. I remember saying "Oh, my God" at one point. Even if I had trained at doing anything, I don't think I could have consciously called on myself to do it. In the second half when it became very intense, the sounds just spontaneously came out of me.

> I think the nurses were surprised but I didn't
> care, and they didn't say anything.
> Carmen

Finding this uninterrupted setting can be challenging. Hospitals, by their very nature, are more prone to medical intervention. Mothers can be disempowered without even realizing it is happening or knowing what to do about it.

> I thought the midwife and doctor were in complete agreement with me but at the hospital, they were making the birth into something different, and I couldn't stop it. It turned out to be a total contrast of what they think is good for you and what you know is best for yourself.
> Lorraine

Home or birthing centers can be the right place for those who choose them. The intimacy and safety of one's home or of a home-like environment can provide the internal assurance of all being well, no matter how it goes. Midwives or doctors who don't interfere with the mother giving birth in her own way while at the same time being skilled in case of complications can help mothers have the peace of mind they need.

> Neither my husband nor I were totally ready for a home birth, but we were sure we did not want to give birth in the hospital. We were fortunate to find a birth center with a really great midwife. I couldn't have asked for more. The birth was everything we had hoped for.
> Teresa

I wanted a home birth, but my partner and parents and friends were all against it. But I knew it was right. I asked my baby, and I knew that he agreed so I did it. And the birth was wonderful. In the end, my partner was very supportive and caring. After the baby was born, he said he would recommend home birth to others.
Eldora

At the same time, with good preparation and a respectful birth team, hospital birth can be the momentous experience it is intended to be.

I had all four of my children in a hospital. The only way I can describe my births is that there is nothing else like it. I was just elated. When my first child was born, the doctor told me to reach down and pull her out, which I did. I will never forget the feeling of love and exhilaration.
Marcella

I had a cesarean birth due to medical reasons. I had to fight to get the doctor to agree to an epidural and a few other things since they were totally new ideas at the time. The doctor was a very big, jolly fellow who clowned around and sang opera during the surgery. It was a relaxed and fun atmosphere for my baby to be born in. She was only one kilo at birth. I had her immediately on my chest after she came out and we bonded beautifully.
Marilena

Each birth is uniquely personal and so are the choices made by parents as to where, how, and with whom to give birth. Tantra Yoga understands that each birth happens according to the shared samskaras* of the infant and parents and that there are no accidents in birth. Everything about birth and family is what we need in this lifetime. Whatever the spectrum of experiences we go through in life, the ultimate purpose is to bring us to truth and love in the greatest sense of the words. Birth is undeniably one of the most profound milestones in that journey.

## Difficult Births: Trauma, Time, & Healing

> Birth trauma happens. One day you will tell your story of how you overcame what you went through and it will be someone else's survival guide.
>
> Unknown

For many reasons, birth can get waylaid and become an experience that leaves mother and baby with mild to severe feelings of emptiness, anxiety, loss, anger, or disconnection from oneself and each other. At times, the acts of disempowerment are so subtle and accepted as normal, that mothers don't acknowledge or trust the upsetting feelings that they are left with. At other times, mothers know something is wrong, but they are in a vulnerable position and may be the only ones sensing the disparity between what is and what ought to be. These unexpressed feelings may not go away after birth but fester in the mother's heart and mind.

---

* Samskaras: reactions to actions, explained more fully in this chapter's section, "Samskara and Birth: All Part of a Bigger Plan."

After the birth, the midwife left. I had to wait several hours until a new doctor came in the morning to stitch the episiotomy. That was the traumatic part. I had been taken away from my baby and was just lying in a room for many hours with other women being wheeled in and out. The feeling of being alone without the baby was horrible. Talking about it even now, 38 years later, it awakens a lot of emotions.

Olenka

Disempowering and helpless experiences anytime during pregnancy, labor, or birth have a strong correlation with disempowered and helpless feelings as a new mother. Lingering and often unacknowledged feelings may result in difficulties bonding with the baby and relationship issues as well as contribute to postpartum depression. A mother may consciously or unconsciously feel like a failure, incapable of doing what other mothers seem to do well and may be blaming herself, with feelings of guilt.

I always felt guilty for what my daughter went through. She was taken from me immediately and I saw her only after 10 hours. Now four-and-a-half years later, I still feel a gap that I don't feel with my son born at home. I only saw her for 40 seconds before they took her, and I missed her terribly in those three days in the hospital. She was given me to breastfeed, of course, but only for short periods.

Madeline

One of the main stumbling blocks in combatting birth trauma is that its existence is not widely recognized. What makes it worse is that people around the mother and baby often don't understand what is happening. "Cheer up," they will say. "It's over now and you have a healthy baby. You should be happy." This grossly undermines a mother's feelings, especially when she has no one to turn to.

> We were separated for many hours after birth. The nurses told me to get some sleep and don't worry, the baby was fine. But I felt that I was supposed to be with my daughter, that she needed me, and I wasn't there. This same feeling surfaces even now when I feel I should have helped her with something more than I did.
> Themis

Zelda had planned a waterbirth in the hospital. She felt like labor was going fine, but the nurses kept asking her if she wanted pain medication and as labor got harder, she eventually agreed. "After the injection I gave up," she remembers. Dilation slowed down and when she finally started pushing, the baby wasn't coming. She was flat on her back, the hardest possible position to push in but the most commonly used in hospitals, for three hours. "My husband and the doctor were standing between my legs discussing the problem like a business meeting, deciding what they should do. I yelled at them to stop talking as if it was an arbitrary event." After several vacuum extraction attempts, she had a cesarean.

> I suppose I feel a kind of anger at myself for not knowing it could have been different. I hold a

> sadness that that's what women are subjected to because they don't know better. It's iniquitous, unnecessary and like we're being robbed. It's so subtle, because it's so easy for women to feel intimidated just being in a hospital. We're shy about our bodies, our nakedness. We feel exposed and then we can't do the work of birth with the same centeredness.
>
> Zelda

It is not just postpartum depression, the "baby blues," or mood and anxiety disorders that may result, but even post-traumatic stress disorder (PTSD.) Britain's Birth Trauma Association explains, "It is now generally accepted that PTSD can be a consequence of a traumatic birth experience." Long-time birth activist and founder of the Birth Crisis Network, the late Sheila Kitzinger, has said, "PTSD can occur after a birth in which a woman felt she had no control over what people did to her and was just a body on the table. She is alert, irritable and panic-stricken. She may feel as if she has been raped. And, as so often with rape, she believes that somehow it must have been her fault. For these women birth was a kind of torture." She goes on to say that this is different from postnatal depression because the birth experience keeps repeating itself in the mother's mind "like a video on a loop. She is constantly reliving the trauma and can't switch it off."

Shannon had a wonderful pregnancy and was looking forward to the birth. When her waters broke and she had no contractions, she was given medication to start labor. Because it was going slowly, the IV drip was increased so often that finally, there were no pauses between contractions, and she was struggling intensely to keep up. She was also on the fetal monitor continuously and wanted to move but was told that she could not. "I was losing control," she so vividly recalls, "and I was terrified." Then the doctor came in and did an internal exam of some sort, though to this day, she doesn't know what or why. Nobody explained it to her. "The pain was already so bad and then he gave me more pain. I was crying and screaming at him to stop but he didn't. He just told me to stop crying and said, 'This will help you.' I didn't feel like a person. That's when I broke down and begged for an epidural."

> After my daughter was born, I was crying a lot and could not settle down and couldn't sleep. But the baby slept all the time. She didn't eat and barely woke up for 3 days. The other babies around were nursing and so on but my baby wasn't. The next day they let me go home and I was so relieved. But I kept having visions, like a movie all the time in my head about the birth — the pain and the doctor doing whatever he did to me and everything. Even when I was pregnant the second time, I saw this doctor in the hospital when I went for a check-up, and I had an immediate reaction. I couldn't breathe just looking at him.
>
> Shannon

> I had a C-section and only realized years later that I went through PTSD after the birth. I started having panic attacks, I cried for days after he was born. I was taking these drugs for pain that were making me vomit and hallucinate. The baby couldn't do anything, he was completely dependent on me. My hormones seemed to be all over the place. I was so overwhelmed with grief and despair that

when I looked at this small baby in my arms,
whom I had to nurse and care for, I just couldn't
connect with him.

Kyra

Kitzinger tells us that a woman who has been through a difficult time in labor is initially in a numb emotional state. She is relieved that it's over but is not yet able to let the emotions fully surface. This can last weeks, months, or years. Then at some point, and often unexpectedly, it all hits her with feelings that are very complicated. "The woman feels bound to be grateful to the professionals who helped her deliver her baby, especially if the baby was considered to be at risk, and yet these are the very people who she feels have violated her. A woman who has had an emergency cesarean can be very vulnerable to this." Acknowledgement of the trauma and supportive care by others can be initial steps to recovery. "What a woman needs," says Kitzinger, "is to be able to talk with someone who understands, a person who does not try to explain or justify the treatment they received, or to criticize them and the way they feel about what happened to them, and who knows how to listen reflectively."

Successive births that are empowering can help some mothers recover though it is not uncommon to go into labor and birth with fears from the previous one. Shannon's second birth was far better than the first. She had become a meditator in the time between births and this helped her to work through some of the triggering feelings. She felt stronger and more prepared. She refused continuous monitoring and insisted on walking, moving, and using the exercise ball. She felt alert and labor was manageable. Though she had flashes of panic during labor from memories of the first birth, she managed to focus and not let the memories derail her. "I realized in the second birth that the pain from the first, with the continuous IV medication inducing labor, was not normal," she recalls. "In the first birth, I was screaming a lot. The nurses had told me to breathe but it was too awful. The second time it hurt but I was okay."

One of the outcomes of trauma at birth is that the oxytocin response is interrupted and the stress system is overly activated. When stress hormones rather than love hormones are dominant in mother and infant, it can be very hard for them to bond. With the right support and safety, this can often be overcome. "Obviously, the most conducive environment for bonding is one in which parents and baby are allowed plenty of time alone together in a warm, relaxed place. But what can you do if those ideal circumstances don't exist?" says Jody Wright in *Parenting from the Heart*. "You can work to recreate these same interactions with a child, whether it is weeks, months, or years later: privacy, touch, eye contact, communication through voice, common biorhythms, breastfeeding or closeness during feeding, sharing of smells and warmth." When this happens, love hormones flow, bonding occurs and both mother and infant begin to heal.

> My first birth was horrible – extremely disempowering, long and to be honest, somewhat devastating. It took us time to get over the shock, both my baby and I. But gradually, we became perfectly connected.
> Zoe

Jennifer Jamison Griebenow, in *Healing the Trauma: Entering Motherhood with PTSD*, suggests that if mama and child play at dramatizing the birth, it can be a very proactive way of rewiring the memories for both. "Wrap yourself and your child in your robe or a warm blanket and talk yourself and your child through your birth experience. When it's time for your baby to be 'born,' open the robe and say to your child just what you would like to have said to him or her at the birth. I have found as the years go by, when cuddling with my cesarean-born son, that we sometimes lapse into baby talk and 'mother talk' almost unintentionally. I hold him close and comment on how beautiful and sweet he is. It sounds a bit funny when explained but each incident, I find, draws us closer, perhaps bringing us another step toward what should have been from the beginning."

Renata has used this play method regularly with her first son, Ilias. His birth was fast, and she ended up being rushed to the hospital while in labor, feeling the need to push but holding back.

> The baby was actually wanting to come when we were in the car and I was pulling in rather than letting him come out and that was traumatizing for both of us. I can see it in him. He often goes towards something pleasurable and then holds himself back.
>
> Renata

"Now he's five and he's become much better, but we've been working on it. When I want him to relax or play together, I often ask him if wants to hear his birth story or another story. Or we might make a cave with blankets, and I'll ask him if he wants to play tigers or play birth. He always chooses birth. Sometimes I tell the story and sometimes he tells the story. I hold him and pretend to be the uterus around him and say, 'This is how you were in my belly.' Then I squeeze like having contractions and he will ask, 'Do I push now?' I tell him no, just wait, you don't do anything yet, just the belly is pushing and contracting and we go through the whole thing and he really likes it. He'll say, 'It was not very good for me because mom was saying *hold on, hold on* and she shouldn't have but she had to.' I ask him usually if he wants to do it the way it was or the way it could have been done better. Sometimes he chooses one and sometimes the other. Whatever way he chooses, finally it is time to push, and he comes out of my squeezing arms and is born."

For mothers and infants like Renata and Ilias whose births did not happen as hoped for or as planned, healing is possible. "I do not wish this opportunity to learn from trauma or pain for anyone," says psychologist Lynn Madsen, author of *Rebounding from Childbirth,* "yet here is the paradox: if such things do happen, then I hope there are gifts from having learned the hard way."

> I don't think I told anybody about how traumatized I felt after birth. This was nearly forty years ago. It wasn't like today when people talk about these things. I was very ashamed of what happened. The second time, I tried not to focus on the memories of the first one and thought it would be different. I think this is what has brought me to my path today of helping other mothers to become empowered.
> Emunah

> My first birth cascaded into a nightmare of interventions that ended up with a C-section. It was that experience that pushed me to become a doula and eventually, a doula trainer in order to support other women to give birth better than I did.
> Maia

"These gifts [that come from learning the hard way] are powerful", Madsen adds, " and they will continue to keep on giving throughout one's life."

# Samskara & Birth: All Part of a Bigger Plan

> All actions, whether introversial or extroversial, crude or subtle certainly lie latent in individuals in seed form as potential reactions. One day they will be expressed in the external world. The reaction of one's action will lie in potential form until the proper time and place arrives for its expression.
>
> P. R. Sarkar, *Science of Action*

As humans, we sometimes plague ourselves with thoughts of why something happened the way it did. We may remember painful or hard situations again and again, sometimes blaming ourselves, sometimes blaming others, sometimes dejected or angry or experiencing any number of feelings. Similarly, we may recall joyous events, going over what made them special in the hopes of them being repeated regularly in our lives. These ponderings are not only normal but a necessary part of our mental/emotional processing. If we didn't retrospectively try to understand what happened, we would not learn from it and move ahead in our lives. The Tantra Yoga concept of *samskara* adds depth to this understanding, helping us have broader, more insightful perspectives on life's challenges and joys.

Karma is a word that means action and samskara means the reaction to past actions. Samskara is intimately tied to the concept of rebirth, i.e., that we incarnate lifetime after lifetime in order to continue working towards our goal of self-realization. In this process, we may act unconsciously, or consciously, in ways that harm others. Or ways that benefit and give joy to others. Whatever our actions are, they will reap corresponding reactions in another lifetime. These reactions are called samskaras.

Samskara has been called one's spiritual DNA, genetically encoding us from a non-physical perspective. We come into each lifetime with inborn samskaras for certain experiences, whether painful or pleasurable, that have to be met and lived through. There are no accidents in major life events such as birth and death, who our children, parents or significant others are, where and in what social circumstances we are born, and so on. The time, place and people of each lifetime have to be precisely right for incarnating souls to experience their samskaras. Sarkar gives the example of a boy named Rama whose samskara was to suffer the pain of losing his father at the age of eleven. For this to happen, Rama had to be born to a father who, according to his own samskaras, had to die when his son was eleven. Likewise, Rama's mother had to have the samskara to lose her husband when he, she and her children were all certain ages. While the intricate complexities of samskaras are far beyond the human mind to comprehend, the key point is that life experiences are not random. Whatever occurs has been reaped from past actions and brings with it opportunities for deep and purposeful growth.

It is important to note here that while samskaras shape many of life's events, how we meet those samskaric experiences is not predetermined. Take Rama, for example. He may turn into an angry, rebellious boy unconsciously seeking to take revenge on the world for the loss of his father. Or he may use the pain of loss to become a more caring, responsible person, even at a young age. It is essentially the extent of one's progress on the journey through lifetimes that sets the stage for how we respond to samskaric occurrences.

Back to birth and samskara. Each birth happens according to the shared samskaras of the infant and parents. Each child is perfectly matched with his or her parents and vice versa. Lessons to be learned, love to be shared — whether it is easy love or hard love – are all part of a bigger picture of life. In the end, it is the deeply intimate bond between mothers and infants that can be a source of strength and insight, allowing them to support each other in whatever way birth unfolds.

Lavanya is a committed activist whose life, apart from caring for her family, could be said to be dedicated to caring for other mothers. She is a pillar of strength for many and has grown deep spiritual roots within herself over the years. Her first birth was a traumatic hospital birth, the next two were good hospital births, and the last was a quietly blissful home birth. Her understanding of samskaras was part of the process of eventually accepting that each birth happened perfectly, exactly as it needed to.

> In my 20's, I didn't know any better, so I gave birth the way I did. Each birth has been a lesson in the work I'm doing now. Like a course that starts out with the introductory 100, next birth 200, 300 and finally 400. Everything happened as it had to, each of them unique and necessary. In the past, I regretted that the earlier births were not "better," but I've left that behind finally knowing that each one was what I needed to be able to help women more, to relate to different ways of giving birth and supporting women in whatever happens to them.
>
> Lavanya

Where our minds are at the time of death has an impact on our rebirth. People who die in intense fear or terror, or in shock as in a sudden accident may be reborn with painful memories needing to be expressed. Sometimes traumatic births create fear and terror because those are the samskaras that need to be lived through. Mandy and Amir had an infant who cried constantly, almost never stopping except when eating or sleeping. Both parents were exhausted and desperate. Talking to them about samskaras helped to relieve their feelings of being inadequate parents. Their son was not crying because they were doing something wrong. He was crying because he was in mental/ emotional pain. He was obviously experiencing a painful samskara but at the same time, the baby had the samskara to be born to loving parents who could help him through it. This understanding gave them space to step back and feel compassion for the pain their son was going through. Talking to Mandy and Amir about listening to babies (see chapter 2) strengthened them in their ability to support their son.

The story of samskaras, though, doesn't stop here. Because every thought and action creates new samskaras, and since samskaras are generally expressed in later lifetimes, we would be trapped inside the cycle of recurring lifetimes forever if there were not a way out. Fortunately, there is a way.

Think of the mind like a soft rubber ball. When we think or act, it is as though an indentation has been made in the surface of the ball. When the reaction to that action occurs, the indentation disappears, and the ball regains its previous shape. Since the ball is always trying to regain its shape, the ultimate goal is to live through all one's samskaras and stop making new ones. The only way to do this is by surrendering the *doership* of actions to Pure Consciousness. The everyday *I* of I think, I act, I want, and so on needs finally to realize that it is the deeper, greater *I* who is thinking, acting, and wanting. The small *I* is a temporary phenomenon with a particular personality, nationality, likes and dislikes, and all the other aspects of identity. But these aspects will all pass with the changing of bodies and lifetimes. It is the greater *I* that remains the same throughout all incarnations and it is that greater *I* that calls us constantly to come home, to merge our small sense of who we are with Its beauty, magnitude, and greatness. Surrendering the doership of actions to that deepest inner self is the key to not collecting more samskaras and ultimately returning to the Source of All That Is.

## Chapter 7

# After-Birth Love

*Childbearing requires an exchange of a known self in a known world for an unknown self in an unknown world.*

Reva Rubin, *Midwifery, Mind and Spirit*

## Who Is This New Me?

Birth is about both mother and baby being born — the baby onto this planet and the mother into motherhood. Both events are dramatic changes and ones for which, most mothers agree, there is little else in life that compares. "As women give birth to children, they, in a sense, birth themselves," says author Vangie Bergum. Mothers and infants are both going through massive changes at the same time. "The milestones in the children are so obvious," noted one mother, "but the mother's profound changes are not as noticeable."

> Motherhood is about opening a whole new door and walking through into an entirely new life and becoming a new person.
>
> Renee

> There's no going back to who I was before
> motherhood. Never will I be that person again.
> Fiona

Sometimes pregnant women express fears or resistance when they hear these sweeping statements. "I don't want to become someone else. I like who I am," a pregnant friend recently said, almost as a plea to prevent the inevitable. The truth is that mothers remain the same and they do not. We will always carry with us the foundational singularity of who we are. Mothering, and in fact, spiritual growth in general, is an emergent process, allowing deeper universal characteristics to permeate our sense of self. The challenge is to see the fears and resistance and surrender them to the newer self. By letting go, we gain more.

> After I had my daughter, I remember thinking
> that I didn't feel like myself and then having the
> realization that I'm not that self and I will never
> be that self ever again. So, I can just stop thinking
> that I don't feel like myself and get to know the
> way I feel because this is who I am now.
> Noriah

Noriah so accurately describes the phenomenon as getting to know "who I am now." Most mothers agree that it is not a frightening unknown self that surfaces. Rather a deeper, kinder, broader self seems to morph from the heart of who one has always been. Though the transformation happens without consciously willing it to, it can be a very conscious and empowering process of observation and mystery, watching oneself think and act in ways unfamiliar until now but common to mothers everywhere. It is something like merging into a universal mothers' consciousness, one that is capable of millions of brilliant, individual expressions.

My mother self is someone I'm happy to meet.
I feel like I've woken up to a more caring me.
And I'm more honest, even about my
weaknesses.
Hannah

My friends tell me that I am so sweet and
different from before. And I feel it. I feel more
tender and caring than I ever imagined I could.
Fiona

Children seem to pull the truth out of those around them.
No more hiding behind appearance, status, belongings, or
talents. Infants and children dive into the personal and previously
hidden nooks and crannies of mama's mind, personality, and self-
identity. Like taking a truth pill. These little ones bring out the
best (and the worst), just for mother to see herself. "The arrival of
a baby is like having a live-in Zen master parachuted into your
home," says mindfulness meditation teacher Jon Kabat-Zinn. "As
any Zen master will do, the infant will push all your buttons. You
will be finding out a lot about yourself that you didn't even know
was there." But the hidden beauty is that they do this without
judgment, with the greatest of love and acceptance, creating lots
of space for reflection and change.

They teach you to look at your life and be aware
of what you're doing, what you're eating, what
you're wearing, they ask you so many questions
and they challenge you a lot.
Hiroko

I feel so responsible as a mother, needing to
teach my children many things and realizing

how much I don't know. I'm seeing life through different eyes. My children have helped me wake up.

Satya

"It's an immensely wonderful opportunity to experience love in a way that has a profound purity to it," says Kabat-Zinn. "You allow yourself to be aware of all the different aspects it is bringing out in you. It's a tremendous period of joy, this kind of awareness of parenting."

The constantly evolving sense of identity as a mother is analogous to Tantra Yoga's concept of self-realization, gradually and inescapably peeling off layers of the self that keep us hidden from our truest self. The process of this transformation involves what Sarkar calls "clash and cohesion." The enormous challenges facing mothers, babies (and spiritual aspirants) push us to our limits again and again, only to bring us to deeper levels of awareness and joy. We emerge as more cohesive beings in all levels of existence. As much as our infants are full of love and acceptance, the Infinite Self bathes us in limitless love, endless acceptance, and irrevocable meaning in the journey of our lives.

## A Mother's Unique Self

Rather than always trying to do the right thing as a parent, you will be more successful in your mission as you discover the right to be.

Vimala McClure, *The Path of Parenting*

So that children will have a greater chance to be who they truly are, a mother's job centers around the awareness of being who she truly is. But becoming a mother doesn't happen overnight. "The birth of a mother does not take place in one dramatic, defining moment but gradually emerges," say husband and wife researchers, Nadia and Daniel Stern. As clearly as the infant is a new person in a new world, mothers are likewise entering completely new territory, perhaps especially true for first time mothers. Too often, mothers feel pressured by expectations or ideals of motherhood that inadvertently sabotage their ability to mother fully. Some mothers feel they are surrounded by people telling them what to do. "People stop me on the street and give all kinds of unwarranted advice, like telling me my baby needs to have a hat on, it's too cold … or she needs to take her hat off, it's too warm!" says Marianna. "I get confused and angry and sometimes don't know what is right." Sometimes mothers are anxious because of the responsibility of caring for this new baby, exacerbated by feeling alone without enough help or support. Still others are knowingly or unknowingly influenced by lingering effects of trauma from the birth of their child or even subconsciously from their own birth, childhood, or other times in life. These and a myriad of reasons can cause a mother to feel incapable or inadequate.

It is crucial to not strive to be like the media images of mothers, the mother next door or even like a friend. "Walking into parenting with the wrong expectations," warn Alisa Volkman and Rufus Griscom in their TED talk, "is what decreases happiness."

> Somehow a myth has been floating around that a good-mom mold exists somewhere out there and that something is wrong with us if we don't fit it. Who invented this good-mom mold and gave it power to control our lives? Your mother? Mother-in-law? The perfect mother in your neighborhood? The negative voice in your

head? All of the above? Nobody really knows the origin of the good-mom mold. Remember, it's a mythical mold. But we sure do know what it looks like and all too familiar is the pressure we feel to fit within its edges.

Morgan & Kuykendall, *Real Moms: Exploding the Myths of Motherhood*

Expectations of "ideal" mothering give way to realizing that mothers are always charting new territory. Pulitzer and Nobel prize winner, Toni Morrison, recounted these feelings about motherhood in an interview with the journalist, Bill Moyers.

There was something so valuable about what occurred when I became a mother. It was the most liberating thing that ever happened. Liberating because the demands that children make are not the demands of a normal "other." And they were not interested in all the things that other people were interested in, like what I was wearing or if I were sensual. Somehow all of the baggage that I had accumulated as a person about what was valuable just fell away. I could not only be me – whatever that was – but somebody actually needed me to be that. If you listen to your children and look at them, they make demands that you can live up to. If you listen to them, somehow you are able to deliver a better self, one that you like. The person that was in me that I liked best was the one my children seemed to want.

Toni Morrison, *Conversations with Toni Morrison*

When a mother has support and a sense of doing her best, she is forging an identity of herself as a mother which is open-ended, in process and uniquely hers. Gradually the mother seed within sprouts and she becomes the mother that only she can be.

> My mother had the idea that she would stop her career and have children and she would be so happy. But she wasn't. Being home with the children didn't satisfy her so I grew up with the idea that mothering was just hard work, sacrifice, and a big disappointment. I had the idea that I might not like being a mother and didn't really look forward to it. But when it happened, I surprised myself by loving it.
> Karina

> My children helped me to become who I am. I have my ideas and my ways of mothering and if someone else doesn't like them well, what does it matter? They're mine. I no longer think about having my ideas negated or laughed at.
> Sondra

> It took me a while, but I finally accepted that my children will always push me into the unknown. There are so many times when I'm unsure if I am doing the right thing, questioning what effect I am having on them for good or bad, feeling sorry that I lost my temper and so on. I struggled with this a lot with my first child but once I accepted it, it was

an amazing relief. And I actually began to feel
that I was doing a better job.
Hiroko

Everyone's entrance into motherhood and journey of love will
be theirs personally. It will never happen that any two mothers and
babies act and react in exactly the same way. Mother and baby are
in an ongoing dance of experiencing from each other how to love.
The experience is felt as "mine" — *my child knows I am her mother,
and she looks to me for love and support in ways that are uniquely and
specially ours.* When her son was born, one mother expressed this
sentiment that so many mothers feel: "I thought he was the most
beautiful baby in the world, that no one was ever going to be that
beautiful." If love flows the way it is designed to, children are
especially beautiful to their mothers and mothers are especially
beautiful to their children. Zoe tells of driving in the car with her
nearly two-year-old son in the back seat. At one point, she looked
at him in the rearview mirror and said, "Victor, you're a beautiful
boy." And he replied, "Momma, beautiful boy." She laughed and
said, "I'm his 'beautiful boy,' too." They are equally beautiful to
each other. Each is sure of the place they have in the other's heart
and their relationship is uniquely theirs and theirs alone.

## Bountiful Mother's Milk

We see the profound relationship between
mother and child summed up in the first act of
an infant on entering the world, which is to
suckle at its mother's breast. What more perfect
lesson in love could there be beyond this
complete dependence matched by total
acceptance and devotion? To me the image of a

mother breastfeeding her baby is the most potent symbol of human love.

Dalai Lama

Surely one of the most exquisite designs of nature is the life-sustaining act of breastfeeding. "We call the one who feeds us, who cradles us close to her body, our whole length pressed into her, Mama, all identified with the Latin mamma, the breast," says researcher Eva Simms. "We 'live from' her and she is the first nourishment, the first experience of enjoyment and happiness."

I was her house, but more than that I was the field that nourished her, the rain that quenched her thirst, the sun that warmed her skin. And it is such a miracle to have seen that small, red, wrinkled creature take in my milk and grow. Milk was the line that tied us together, the very special stuff that gave her life, growth, and contentment.

Eva Simms, *The Child in the World: Embodiment, Time, and Language in Early Childhood*

Breastfeeding, for some women, is one of life's exceptional experiences.

There is absolutely nothing like breastfeeding. I cannot begin to describe how it is. Deeply loving, it epitomizes an exceptional exchange of everything that love has to offer.

Akila

Breastfeeding was one of the most incredibly blissful times in my life. Nothing can compare to

it. It's physical, instinctual, emotional, aesthetic, intimate, and transcending. It makes your baby feel extraordinarily happy and safe. You are nurturing this person fully, your heart is open and you have an incredible capacity to comfort.
Alexandra

I just loved breast-feeding. For me it was deeply satisfying, sweet and connecting. I loved the feeling of it and the sound of it and the fact that my body knew exactly how much milk to make all by itself.
Ziina

During breastfeeding when I can truly be present with my daughter, it's as though time stands still. It is only the two of us.
Lena

"A newborn baby has three demands," wrote the late birth activist Grantly Dick Read, "warmth in the arms of mother, food from her breasts and security in the knowledge of her presence. Breastfeeding satisfies all three."

When the letdown reflex occurs, it is just amazing. There's an energetic connection between mother and baby even if you're not in the same room or even if you're 10 km away. If the baby woke up and needed to be fed, my body would let me know. I found that so incredible. In the middle of the night my

breasts would wake me up about five minutes before my baby did.
Abia

When I took my first daughter to the doctors for her checkup and she had gained weight, maybe a pound, I thought, "She did that from my milk!" It seemed like a miracle. I'll never forget that feeling. It was so amazing and so deep.
Lavanya

It is one of life's contemporary challenges that so many infants are not breastfed and so many mothers are regularly convinced that they are not capable of breastfeeding. "Not enough milk," "Too much trouble", or "Formula is easier and more nutritious" are some of the usual reasons offered to convince mothers to bottle feed their infants. In some cases, it is truly not possible to breastfeed, but those cases are fewer than most people realize. Even mothers of adopted children are able to stimulate their body to produce milk and can at least partially breastfeed.

That said, many mothers give up or don't start because of high levels of stress and lack of support. Many times it is not because the mother doesn't want to. When she runs into problems, she doesn't know what to do or who to turn to for help. It can be much harder in the beginning than many mothers expect and that can be discouraging, physically, mentally, and emotionally.

I did need support at the beginning both times. Even though I'd learned a lot in between my babies, I still needed some support the second time as well as the first.
Ramona

The first three days were so difficult. My nipples were sore and the baby wasn't latching on right and the milk hadn't come in yet. That's when many women feel like giving up, but I was lucky that I had supportive friends who helped. On the third day when the milk came in, my breasts swelled up and were hard and it actually felt terrible. I didn't know that it was going to smooth out and get really easy very soon after that. I remember thinking in those first days, "Oh my god, is this what this is about? This is not nice." But then very quickly afterwards from day four or five it became absolutely perfect.

Zoe

I tried to breastfeed both my children, but the babies were crying, they obviously were not being fed enough and I didn't have anyone to help me. If I knew then what I know now, I would have gotten support and would probably have been able to do it.

Marcia

Many societies have not completely accepted breastfeeding and mothers may face a lot of obstacles from friends and families as well as in public. But countless breastfeeding mothers agree that the obstacles pale in comparison to the benefits and the joys.

It was such a beautiful experience with both of them. It's not without its challenges but I don't think those challenges are more than if the baby is fed artificially. For me, it's been so central to our relationships.

Regan

No one in my family breastfed and neither did my friends. But I kept remembering about my grandmother in Sicily who had breastfed all her children. I was really alone in breastfeeding. It wasn't like I had friends whom I would meet and we would breastfeed together. I was quite isolated, but in some ways, I liked it. It was just me and my baby. Nowadays it's changed very much, and I see women breastfeeding more easily out in public, stopping on the bench in the park to breastfeed. It makes me feel very happy.

Lavanya

An important closing note is that extolling the value of breastfeeding does not at all denigrate the love and efforts needed to feed babies with formula. Sometimes mothers feel shamed or guilty when discussions about breastfeeding arise. That is not the intention here. Formulas are lifesavers, of course, when they are needed. Sometimes breastfeeding is not possible, more than one person needs to feed the baby, or formula is simply the mother's choice. There are many reasons to give formula to infants who will grow and thrive. After all, it is the love between mother and infant that is the crux of the matter in any scenario.

# Expect the Unexpected: The Only Constant in Life Is Change

Everything which exists in the universe will certainly have to undergo change.

P.R. Sarkar, *Sadvipra, Taraka Brahma, Sadashiva and Shrii Krsna*

Whatever a mother's situation is, the duality inherent in life often creates a myriad of fluctuating feelings and states of mind. The awe and beauty inspired by the newborn co-mingle with uncertainty and fatigue, sometimes loneliness and anxiety and a host of other expected and unexpected newness. Mothers may feel that something is wrong if they are not constantly flooded with loving emotions, an unrealistic and untenable expectation. They may feel they are not doing it right if the baby has colic, the laundry is perennially unfolded, or the dark circles under their eyes seem to grow larger by the day. Fluctuating hormones may cause mood changes and the enormity of 24-hour, never-ending care can be overwhelming. "There are no words to describe the intensity of what a mother feels or what she is achieving as a mother," says author Naomi Stadlen. "The essentials of mothering are invisible. A mother may be exhausted and her home may look chaotic, yet she may be doing wonderfully well as a mother."

Many cultures emphasize the first forty days after birth, or twenty-one days as suggested by Sarkar, as a time to limit activities so that mother and baby can focus on being together, ideally being cared for by others as much as possible. These immediate post-birth days are seen as a special, inner, recuperative, and almost retreat-like period. Birth is an upheaval and a shock, even the best of births, and though some mothers feel energetic and ready to go as soon as the baby is born, the body and mind know that they need time to recover and integrate what has happened. This period facilitates the settling in of the new soul in the infant's body and the beginning of the mother's body and mind adjusting to a post-birth state. More importantly, it is time for mother and baby to get to know each other.

> After the birth of my first son, I was in a little bubble with the baby and my husband. Nothing else in the world mattered at all. I have never been so disinterested in what was going on beyond our own home. It seemed so very instinctual to be that way. A similar thing happened the second time. I did feel like I was in a bubble, but the difference was that we had a three-year-old in the bubble. It put some pressure on my husband, I think, because he had to keep things going while I was in that bubble.
> Ramona

> I remembered hearing about women in India who don't get out of bed for forty days and people take care of everything for them and I thought that if I had that, I'd be okay. I was alone most of the time. I had to get up to do the laundry and cook and all these things. The worst part was about the first three weeks. After that, it began slowly to get better.
> Kate

> I felt so happy and so grateful for that first month. I was mindful of not wanting to see many people or not letting them stay long. It

was the middle of winter and there were storms outside, and it was dark early, and we just settled into being together.

Noriah

Whether or not such a period of quietness and care is possible, the enormity of the expected and unexpected changes after birth make an indelible and never forgotten impression in most mothers' minds.

After birth, I felt like I'd been run over by a truck. That was when reality hit. I just thought the baby would be out and it would be perfect. I was totally exhausted, and I had to feed this child and he was eating constantly. He seemed to eat all day. I felt like the birth had been so hard I needed a vacation, and it was just beginning! On the other hand, I really fell in love with my son during pregnancy. After he was born, it was an intensely strong love like nothing I had ever experienced. It's hard to explain but it was surely the love that not only kept me going but that made me a mother and a better person.

Louisa

After birth with both of my children, I had a very hard time. My first child had colic every afternoon and I couldn't deal with that. My second child didn't want to sleep during the day and one day I was so tired, I turned on the

faucet and he calmed down. I wondered if I would need to run the water all the time!
Sabine

Nobody told me how physically drained I would feel after birth, how misshapen my body would still be and how long it would take to heal. I really had to struggle with this for a long time. But then, when I forgot about it and just paid attention to my daughter, it was all worth it and I even knew I'd do it again.
Amalia

Expected and unexpected change are states which become so fixed as to be normal in a mother's life. The rapid growth of children creates a perennial field of newness and unfamiliarity. That everything is always changing is a spiritual truth mothers become adept at through trial, error, and love. As children push a mother's boundaries, she understands that stability and security are inner assets, that nothing outside of herself can ever be 100 percent stable or predictable. "It's a continuous experimentation, in a good way. I have to become always more open and patient and inventive," said a mother of three. "I also need to rely on a stronger sense of self than I ever knew I had. I can handle much more now than before I was a mother."

A law of quantum physics that has great relevance to a mother's life (and life in general) goes like this:

Life's most challenging existential problems exist outside the expected and the familiar, outside the given rules, beyond past experience, beyond what we know how to handle. In chaos theory, "the edge" is the border between order and chaos, between knowing comfortably what we are about and being totally lost. It is the place where we can be at our most creative. Today, we all have to live at the edge whether we like it or not.

Danah Zohar and Ian Marshall, *Spiritual Intelligence*

Tantra Yoga portrays stability while "on the edge" as an inner asset, not dependent on external circumstances. This is the human side of spiritual growth at its best, necessitating continuous effort combined with stepping back to watch it happen. It is truly this edge which expands hearts and minds, creating changes that are reflected chemically and biologically. But it is the long-term opening of the heart that is the extraordinary outcome.

## Intuition Travels on Love: Heart Communication

(Mother-child interaction) opens a factor called intuition, the ability to perceive information … before it presents itself on the physical level. The mother who has bonded with her infant can do precisely that. It opens up intelligences, capacities, abilities, and powers in her in that she didn't previously have.

Joseph Chilton Pearce, *Reaching Beyond the Magical Child*

Joanna had a dream that her five-year-old daughter, Mandy, had caught her thumb in the door. Just at the moment she was dreaming this, her daughter woke up crying. Joanna quickly asked her, "What's the matter?" Mandy sobbed through tears while holding up her thumb, "My finger! My finger!"

How did they communicate? And what really happened? Did Joanna tap into her daughter's dream state? Were deeper levels of their minds communing while their conscious minds were asleep?

Love spans many realms and communication within a loving relationship takes many forms. Gut-level feelings, knowing something without knowing how we know it, sensing the deeper meaning underneath someone's words or actions, an instantaneous flash of insight … all are forms of intuitive knowing that most of us have experienced. The more we recognize them, the more we realize that they are not so uncommon. They come from a realm deeper than the intellect, beyond thoughts, logic, and memory. According to Sharon Franquemont, a teacher in the graduate program on intuition at the John F. Kennedy University, greater intuitive experiences happen between people in love. "Intuition thrives in the space of love and caring," she says. "Intuition travels on love."

A mother's love is enormous and so is an infant's. And since the infant is as yet immersed in an undifferentiated intuitional love, this positively impacts mama's deeper sensibilities. Love creates a subjectivization of, or a taking into oneself, the vibrational essence of another. It is a heart communication which allows for a dialogue between deeper places of the mind within which intuition exists. Mothers and infants are reading each other intuitively through their bodies, thoughts, feelings and heart-to-heart closeness.

The heart's electromagnetic field, particularly in close proximity but even at a distance, has a measurable impact on those near us. When mothers and babies are able to let love flow, there is a striking parallelism and coherence of not only heart rates but all bodily systems, including brain waves. When mama and baby look at each other and smile, their heartbeats synchronize to each other within milliseconds. They go into the same frequency, heart-brain waves match and there is no dissonance. This not only feels good to both, but it also relieves stress and anxiety and opens the doors for intuition to sweep between the two.

Many years ago, Dr. J. Andrew Armour made the fascinating discovery that the physical heart has its own independent nervous system, later labeled the "heart brain." Intricately complex and amazingly autonomous, the heart-brain can sense stimuli and makes decisions independent of the cranial brain. The heart and the head are in constant communication, but the heart appears to send many more messages to the brain than vice versa. Studies by the HeartMath Institute confirm that the heart senses future events before the brain does. This unique heart sensing seems to be centered in intuition.

When we talk about intuition and the heart in yogic terms, it is not the actual physical heart we are referring to but rather a subtler, vibrational presence in the chest around the heart and lungs. Within this area exists a psychic organ called pránendriya. The word pránendriya comes from the Sanskrit words "prana" and "indriya" which roughly mean "vital life force" and "organ." It is an organ in the subtle or energetic body that intuitively senses subtler characteristics of people or things, often referred to as the sixth sense.

> With the help of this pránendriya, one feels that a particular person is very kind and affectionate or unkind and antipathetic. Such an experience is based more on a subjective feeling than on any outer objective correlation.
> P.R. Sarkar, *Mind, Pranendriya and Vritti*

Pránendriya pulsates with the rhythm of the breath and is receptive only when the breath is calm, as in mind-body coherence or a meditative state. A mother can train herself to create this harmony through conscious awareness of her breath, body, and states of mind, but the infant is completely unable to do that. Of course, no mother can be in a coherent state all the time. And no baby, either. Life is full of stressors and infants need to learn, through mother's touch and closeness, how to come back to a place of coherence when it is lost. Life is not about staying in mental or emotional balance all the time, but rather about returning when we've fallen out. Mama's personal efforts to self-regulate set the stage for baby to learn this and help mum to strengthen it as default mode.

But there are deeper reasons and uses for intuition. Experiences such as Joanna's dream with her daughter only scrape the surface of the vastness of intuition and generally come from the lower levels of intuitive awareness. Though there is great value, of course, in these types of intuitive knowing, their real value lies in awakening our thirst for something deeper. To become absorbed in the universal Oneness requires more than intuition about human love. In its breadth, intuitional practices such as meditation focus the mind to a pinnacled awareness of Consciousness as life itself. We not only recognize the ground of being but also humbly understand our place and purpose in it. The essence of dharma (one's purpose in life), according to Sarkar, lies in intuition.

> When the mind transcends the barriers of intellect the realization dawns in human beings that they cannot reach the abode of the Supreme through material science or philosophy but through intuition alone. Supreme blessedness lies in the unfoldment of intuition.
>
> P.R. Sarkar, *The Ascent of Mind*

# Beyond Human Love: What Next?

> What I cry out for, like every being, with my whole life and all my earthly passion ... is to lose oneself in the unfathomable, to plunge into the inexhaustible, and to give of one's deepest to that whose depth has no end.
>
> Pierre Teillhard De Chardin, *quoted from Ursula King's Spirit of Fire: The Life and Vision of Teilhard de Chardin*

Love in its fullest forms is uniquely personal. If love doesn't touch the human heart in ways to cause enormous challenges, seemingly endless questions, and dramatically transformative changes, then it has not been embraced for the purpose it exists. While mother-infant love may be an unparalleled example of human love, its defining essence is only to show us that love exists, and to prime us to long for more. Human love opens our minds and hearts to love but it is always impermanent, at times disappointing and never able to fill the deepest of all yearnings. Attempting to fill a limitless yearning with anything limited is futile at best, devastating at worst.

The saying that, "In every living being is the thirst for limitlessness" implies an innate drive to progress, to move forward, to endlessly search until we have found an ultimate fulfillment. Wanting to travel to further and further distances catalyzed human inventiveness, resulting in trains and planes. Looking at the sky at night aroused our wonder and yielded astronomy and space travel. Asking the big questions about life and its meaning gave rise to ever-expanding philosophical theories. But all these accomplishments, as valuable as they are, are limited by the very mindsets that created them.

It is a transcendent, infinite love that sustains and nourishes. All of life is about relationships and spirituality is no different. The ultimate personal relationship is with the infinite Beloved. *My Beloved Self and I are in love. Our ever-growing relationship is personal, intimate and uniquely ours.* The sense of a special "mineness", when applied by one's small *I* to one's Infinite *I*, allows for a relationship of growing and enduring love in which the human mind and heart thrives.

As mother-infant love may be innate but does not always flourish due to many different factors, so may spiritual love remain dormant. As any relationship requires ongoing attention and perseverance to let it thrive, so the love with one's Beloved cannot be taken for granted. The relationship we as individuals have with the Infinite is one that must be learned, practiced, and kept in our hearts as one of — nay, as *the* — major life priority. This love seems at times tangibly within our grasp and at other times, so elusive. Once tasted, one can never give up on this love, though it may at times be a hard master, much as mothering children never stops being challenging. It takes one continuously into uncharted waters and forces the soul to navigate through dark and narrow tunnels, ultimately transcending the duality of my Beloved and I. As mother love changes us in every way, making us better people, so Infinite Love seeps into our being, permeating our thoughts and actions with a quiet knowing. And as for joy, there is hands down nothing comparable to the sweetness of Infinite Love's personal transcendent touch. In the end, there is only the Beloved as our soul merges into infinity. Tantra Yoga unequivocally embraces the truth that the only real progress in life and the only lasting joy comes from merging with the limitless self in the most personal, steadfast, and loving way.

The reality is that our infants and children may help us to realize that this is what we are here for.

## Chapter 8
# Children Raising Parents

*The value of marriage is not that adults produce children but that children produce adults.*
Peter de Vries, *Ayurvedic practitioner*

## Mother-making

Our children, even infants before and after birth, are here to teach us as much as we are here to teach them. This is such an important concept that, unlike much of the rest of this book, we're not focusing it primarily on infants and the primal period. We're looking at the whole period of childhood, the most intensely formative years in the parent-child partnership.

There is hardly a mother anywhere who would not immediately admit that her children have taught her a huge amount and made her a better person. Nonetheless, in most cultures, this is seen as something of a side effect rather than a mutual give-and-take. Parenting is viewed as a top-down process. But what happens from the bottom up? What are children's hearts, thoughts, and actions aiming to teach us every day? There's no doubt that parents work hard to raise and care for their children. But perhaps children are working just as hard to raise and care for their parents.

My teenage daughter, Dana, sometimes talks about having raised me as a mother. She's not joking, she's quite serious. One time I had done something for her but had not thought it through well and the situation ended up poorly. I will never forget how she looked at me as a parent would look at a child, shrugged her shoulders and said, "Well, I did the best I could." I have to say she was right.

Maia

In all fairness, we need to create a whole new narrative that validates children for raising their parents equally as much as their parents raise them, albeit in very different ways. It would benefit us all greatly if the idea of being reared by our children were as commonly accepted as the other way around. A quick look at any bookstore shows shelves or online pages filled with books on parenting and raising children but very few, if any, on children raising parents.

I suggest that we coin a new term for this. There are several words that connote the immaturity of childhood as opposed to the maturity of age, such as girl and woman, boy and man, child and adult – but there isn't a corresponding word for a child that relates to the concept of "parent."

The word *parent* comes from the Latin *parere* meaning to bring forth, give birth to, or to produce. Certainly children are giving birth to adults as mothers and parents, starting even in pregnancy. In this book, as we are looking at mothering, we will use the term "mother-maker," at least until something better shows up. Suffice it to say that "parent-maker" or "father-maker" are just as appropriate since so much of this certainly relates to fathers, as well.

> My daughter made me a mother. I wasn't motherly before. I remember when she was only a few weeks old and she was waking me every hour. I was tired and didn't want to wake up. But I had to, and I realized that she was making me be a mother.
>
> Maro

## Children as Teachers

> Sooner or later our children let us know that they arrived in the world with agendas of their own. While we have tremendous influence in the way they express and live out their agendas, we cannot mold and control them. They have as much to teach us as we want to teach them, and the wise parent realizes this early on.
>
> Vimala McClure, *Path of Parenting*

Themis related that while her husband was always seeking to understand himself and life better, she had never had this urge until she had children. "I thought I knew who I was," she admitted, "but my daughters made me realize I didn't." Feeling that her ability to love had grown, not in a theoretical way but in a very grounded and everyday real way, she ended by saying, "How did that happen? My children brought me to this."

Children, in their wisdom, want to ground us in the deepest truths of life so that we will create for them the environment that they need to fully unfold. "Children, in their sweet innocence," one mother said, "seem to want their mothers to expand and unfold as well." Perhaps their every action, gesture and smile are designed, at least in part, to pull us inward towards truth, integrity, and love.

> Having children is a marvelous tool to get you out of yourself, to put other people first, to go through suffering for someone else. They taught me about touch and love, how to be more communicative, more perceptive. It's definitely an education in yourself that is irreplaceable.
> Dana

> Seeing the pure compassion that she just naturally held was a big revelation for me. Big. It helped me understand an ideal that I had only sort of heard about but never experienced.
> Marilena

> With children, you are meeting yourself through all the emotions there are — strong and disappointing, not having patience and feeling inadequate, joy and love, happiness and calm. The clashing and joining of oneself with the children makes the whole experience of life a reality. Through this reality I have grown into who I am and my children have grown into who they are.
> Eliora

> You develop all these capacities and qualities as a mother — empathy, putting others first and sensitivity. They permanently affect your character. When your children grow up, you

don't stop being the person you've become through mothering them. It permanently changes you. I certainly was never the same after that.

Anna

They teach you so much. They teach you to love, to accept, to be grateful. They teach you everything. Really everything. You think you know so much and then you have a child, and everything is much more real and intense.

Maia

Children mother-make in many ways, of course, but the first and foremost is through a purely open heart. Joseph Chilton Pearce, in his introduction to Tobin Hart's book, *The Secret Spiritual Life of Children*, tells of a five-year-old girl asking her father, "Do you know why children are sent into the world? To teach adults to think in their hearts so that everything goes right. Otherwise, they think in their heads and life is hard."

My son is so loving all the time, no matter what. He smiles at everybody anywhere and that impressed me a lot. I found myself trying to see people who are difficult for me through his eyes. I've changed a lot and am more compassionate.

Dora

Sometimes we think we are here to teach children, but I've learned more from her or at least as much. Am I wiser because I have more life experience to offer? In some ways, yes, but

in many ways, no. She lives in her heart. She is constantly amazing me with the depth of connection and innate wisdom she has that doesn't have to be learned.
Noriah

I was incapable of loving anybody until I had a child. My capacity for expressing love and being demonstrative and just feeling it, just accessing it, was much more expanded after my daughter was born. There's no question that her birth made an enormous difference in my ability to love.
Maro

Many mothers speak of how the inherent joy in children helps them in times of stress.

There are moments with children that are like instant relaxation or instant bliss moments. If I am worried or anxious about something, I try to focus fully on them, play with them, feel their smiles and laughter and they make me feel better.
Rhea

Sometimes during the day, I watch my boys being in the moment as they play together and thereby try to center myself as well and be in the moment with what I do.
Margot

They just help you to appreciate the world around you. Sometimes if I'm in a down state, I look over at them, watch them a few minutes and see how they are connected to the earth. It brings me to a different place, helps me to be grateful for what life has given.

Diana

For children to teach us, we have to listen. When children are listened to and their views respected, they are much more likely to show us what they need because they have learned to think their own thoughts, formulate their own opinions, express themselves confidently and then try it all out in the laboratory of the world. "Because you have acknowledged the mutual respect between you and your children," notes Margot, "you cannot help but realize that you are both teaching and guiding each other."

I feel a deep sense of respect for my son. He naturally requires that we listen carefully to his needs. He is not yet two, but his communication is very clear. And consequently, he cries very little. It feels like an equal relationship, where the power is in balance. We are not so much parenting him but listening to him show us the way.

Zoe

Yahaira's second son realized around the age of three that his mother was vegetarian and his father was not. He asked his father why he ate meat and his mother why she didn't. "What is meat?" he asked. His father told him that it was healthy and helps you grow and so on. His mother told him that the animals are innocent, and we don't want to kill them. He would ask about fruits, is it not killing them to cut them and eat them? He would ask about vegetables and cutting trees or plants in the yard. He asked these questions every day. His father started becoming impatient, but the boy didn't stop. Then suddenly after three months, he announced one day, "I am vegetarian like my mom." He said he didn't want to kill the animals. His parents accepted his decision and now, as a teenager, he is still vegetarian.

Listening to children is very often a learned skill. Many or most of us were not brought up being truly listened to and consequently, we don't know how to do it very well. Babies and children are capable of understanding much more than we had previously imagined. Rather than shielding them from life's everyday problems, what they long for is learning how to face them and find a balance between the good and the bad, the hard and the easy, the pleasure and the pain. If we have not been exposed to the idea of listening to children when we have babies, it is never too late to start, as Gwendolyn's story shows.

Gwendolyn and her husband divorced when her daughter, Pam, was around four. The year before they separated was very hard. They tried not to show the discord in front of Pam, but children intuitively sense, in their bodies and without words, what is happening in the parents. Gwendolyn says that one day she was feeling really upset with her husband. All day she tried her best to act normally with Pam but inside she was distraught. That night, when Pam was going to bed, she very softly and compassionately looked in her mother's eyes and said, "You know, sometimes mommies are crying inside." Gwendolyn nearly did cry when she heard that. It opened the door for them to talk about what was happening. Pam was also hurting and needed to be helped to face the pain she felt. Gwendolyn realized after Pam told her one day, "Mommy, you're breaking my feelings" that she needed to be more honest and more aware of how this was affecting her daughter.

Though children have a keen, intuitive sense of what they feel and need, they are not always able to express it. Sometimes it just takes a word or a look or a question to elicit from them what they don't really know how to say. Over time, when they know mama is doing her best to listen and really cares, when they are helped to recognize and give names to emotions and feelings, communication becomes easier.

When Jorg was around two and a half, he went through a period of often hitting other children. One day at the playgroup that he and his mother Rhyana attended, Jorg hit nearly every child there. Rhyana plus all the other mothers tried this and that but Jorg seemed unable to control himself. Jorg was Rhyana's first child, and she didn't really know what to do. Later that day, she sat with him and asked him directly, "What do you need to stop this hitting?" His immediate, unhesitating answer was, "More kisses." Rhyana was stunned. "Do you mean that if I give you more kisses, you will not feel the need to hit others?" "Yes," was his instant reply. That was all she needed to hear. From then on, she bathed him in hugs and kisses and realized how much her frantic schedule kept her from giving him the affection he craved. There was no more hitting after that, thanks to Jorg's mother-making.

## Dharmic Qualities Children Teach Us

> Start off with the intention of knowing who this baby is [i.e. who your children are] and appreciate the adventure of finding out. It's an immensely wonderful opportunity to experience love in a way that has a profound purity to it.
>
> Jon Kabat-Zinn, *Interview with Kidscare Canada*

In a previous chapter, we talked about dharma or living true to the purpose of existence. That means striving to inculcate the essence of Pure Consciousness in every aspect of life. A lofty goal, no doubt, but one which children have the capacity to help with by teaching what could be called heart qualities, those that come from and go back to love as the base. These qualities have immense depth. No matter how much we have grasped their import, we always have more to learn, understand and internalize at a deeper level. Children are wonderful at teaching these qualities and at the same time, their deeper selves very much want to have them reinforced through our example.

The aim here, it is important to say, is not to be a "perfect" mother, always patient, wise, or free from anger. The aim is to be as authentic, honest, and heartfelt as possible, letting our children do their job in helping that happen.

There are many dharmic qualities mothers grow into. Here are just a few.

## Patience

> I had to become a mother to learn compassion, to learn patience, to be accepting and tender. Otherwise, I might never have done it. You have to learn those things as a mother.
> Chantal

Tantra Yoga notes that progress in any sphere of life requires time, determination, and patience. In fact, patience is the first necessary characteristic of those following the path of dharma. Sarkar tells us that, "While in danger, one's great quality is patience." Children are marvelous teachers of patience.

> Patience and acceptance are the biggest lessons
> of mothering. This is not a project that you can
> give up one day. You cannot run away. When
> the times come when you feel you want to run
> away, you have to go back and try to enjoy what
> you're doing.
> Yahaira

Many mothers, when asked what they have been taught by their children, will immediately say "patience." Adult patience can be tested and stretched deciding when, how, and whether to go into a children's world with them or be frustrated by it.

Athina laughingly and yet seriously tells the story of how her firstborn, Grace, taught her patience and acceptance right from the moment of birth. She recalls that after a long, hard labor, she was pushing and it seemed to be taking so long. Comparing it to the feeling of being on the edge of a cliff just about to fall off, she remembers saying to her infant, "OK, you have taught me patience. I have been in labor many hours and I don't think I can go on. But I know that I will. I wondered during pregnancy if I have what it takes to raise you, and now I know that I'll be able to do whatever I need to as a mother. Now I understand. I get the message. So please come out!" Athina totally surrendered and that was a very critical turning point. After that, the baby started coming out. As she was crowning, the midwife said, "Oh, she has a lot of black hair." Athina had always thought that her daughter would be very fair and probably not have much hair as an infant and she remembers saying out loud, "Come out! I love you just the way you are!"

Athina pauses, reflecting on the four years since Grace was born. "Many times, I remember these moments and these thoughts." She says that her daughter has an opinion about almost everything and cannot be pushed to do things except in her own time. "Very often, I remember feeling that desperation when I literally said to her, 'You are teaching me patience and acceptance. I love you just the way you are.' I hear and feel myself back at the birth. I stop and realize how much she is teaching me all the time."

## Humility

> They constantly push your limits. Either you pretend that you know everything or you admit that you don't know anything. Motherhood is a very humbling experience.
> Sarala

Yvonne says that her first child was quiet and mild-mannered. She would sometimes look at other parents when their children seemed overly willful or demanding and feel that she and her husband were doing a much better job at parenting. Then her daughter was born, and this child was very different. Yvonne regularly found herself in situations like those in which she had judged other parents. "I realized how mistaken I'd been. I felt very humbled."

Humility is not about false modesty nor is it hiding ourselves in the background because we feel afraid or inferior. Humility is a trait cultivated through repeatedly recognizing the power of the Great and surrendering to the Consciousness within. It is about realizing ever more deeply over time that it is not our limited *I* doing anything but rather our limitless self.

> You must be more humble than the grass ... as a blade of grass may lie on the ground underfoot, but does not, through its remaining humble, lose its importance ... and more

tolerant than the trees … which, even while being cut, continue to give their cool shade.

P.R. Sarkar, *Safeguards against the Defects of Jinana and Karma*

Listening to and being guided by our children can really humble us. We often sincerely think that we know what is best for them and, of course, there are times when we do. But there are other times when we don't.

Caroline was very bonded with her daughter, and they had a good, communicative relationship. But when Melissa was about nine years old, a new girl moved to the small, rural town they lived in. The girl was from a big city and had very different ways. Caroline thought it was best that Melissa not be too influenced by her. Whenever Melissa asked if she could invite this girl over to play, Caroline always had some excuse or another to say no. Finally, one day Melissa said, "Mom, I know that you always say 'no' because you think she will be a bad influence on me. But maybe I can be a good influence on her." Caroline was speechless. After a pause, she frankly said, "I'm sorry, Melissa. You're right. I haven't been trusting you. Go ahead and invite her over." The girls became close friends. Melissa and her family did, in fact, influence her new friend in a very positive way and she loved spending time at their house. Caroline says that of all Melissa's friends, it was this girl who stayed in touch long after Melissa had grown up and moved away from home.

> Saying, "I'm sorry" to a child during a trying situation is a humbling, respectful experience. It is not a sign of one's diminishing mothering ability. It is a sign that you respect your child's perceptions and knowledge.
>
> Margot

Rhea, quoted earlier in the chapter about going to play with her children when she feels worried or anxious, offered these thoughts. "I have to let them help me feel better," she says. "If I don't stop and tune in to them, if I don't go to them humbly in the spirit of letting them help me, it doesn't happen, and I just stay hanging on to the worry."

I think it is safe to say that no mother is always in tune with herself and her children enough to intuit everything in a timely way. The demands of everyday life can make mothers feel overwhelmed or out of touch. That's to be expected. It is humbling to make mistakes and learn from them. Children's love has the capacity to help with humility because no matter what, they love you just the same.

> They let you start over. If they show you something in yourself you want to change, you can. And they are happier because of it.
> Carmen

## Control of Anger

Tantra Yoga tells us that once anger overtakes us, we are lost. In battle, the one who can remain free from anger will be victorious as those consumed with anger will not be able to think or act clearly. When the nerves become strongly vibrated and trembling, it can take a long time for the body and the mind to calm down again.

Of course, Tantra Yoga also notes that anger is an inborn tendency. Everyone has it. Some tendencies are inborn and some are acquired, but anger is innate. That means that it is always there ready to come to the fore. That also means that it has a purpose and a use. Trying to get rid of something inborn is foolish and a waste of time. The force behind anger can be used to take strong determination to not repeat a certain nagging mistake or to firmly decide to look more deeply into ourselves for the source of understanding. Anger as a strong emotion can be transformed into tremendous compassion when we are able to see the person we are angry with — even if it is ourselves — as someone in pain. By so doing, we call on the mothering instinct, the desire to nurture and give care instead of berate or conquer. Anger directed towards social injustice can propel us to take positive social action. Anger in itself is not harmful. It is how we let it control us that can be harmful.

> I once heard someone say that when we get furious, we should get curious. This implies that we need to dig into the roots of our being to determine its source before it is our undoing.
> Margot

Through meditative practices, we may learn to surrender the anger to its true higher source. We need to step back for a moment, see the bigger picture, breathe, redirect our feelings, and search within to find the capacity to remain calm under provocation.

> Meditation has helped me with anger by helping me to see how it affects my children. Sometimes when I am feeling angry, I realize that I am not angry at my children but at the feelings inside myself. I learned to look at my children when I began to shout and saw them looking confused or hurt, especially the young ones. When I am able to really see them at that moment, it helps me to calm down.
> Hiroko

> Since I've begun meditating, when I start to get
> angry, I am thinking about what I will gain
> from the anger or what is its purpose and so on.
> My children and I discuss these things
> Themis

Everyone has certain tendencies that are their particular challenges. Anger may be extremely challenging for one person but not for another. Even mild anger may be a particular challenge if we were not helped to deal with anger well as children. And even long-time meditators or spiritually minded people may be troubled with anger.

> I don't usually shout at my child. But one day,
> I was very stressed, very tired, and on the verge
> of sickness. I lost control and started shouting
> at my four-year-old. But she didn't react at all.
> She just looked at me and said, "Mama, do you
> really want to talk to me that way?" She
> brought me to my senses. I said, "No, thank
> you." Instead, I knelt down and gave her a big
> hug. Truly, just holding her made me feel so
> much better.
> Artemis

Another mother says that when she and her husband argue, their small child tells them not to do that, don't shout, even when they are not yet shouting but their voices are getting louder. It helps them to calm down. Yet another mother laughingly reports that she does not yell or shout around her six-month-old infant son because when she does, he just laughs, as if to bring her back to her senses.

When my oldest son was small, I would get angry or frustrated more than I do now. Just as I'd start yelling, I'd hear myself saying, "I can't take it anymore!" My son got into the habit of responding calmly with, "No, mum, you can take more." It started to become a habit for me to hear him say that inside myself and it helped me to switch moods before the anger took over.
Rhyana

Eli was a preschool teacher. She worked in a small group setting with around ten to fifteen children and two teachers. Normally, the classroom dynamics were quite flowing. But one day it was overly chaotic, and nothing seemed to bring balance. Try as she might to stay calm, she was just about to spiral out of control and start shouting when one of the three-year-olds came up to her. He didn't say a word but had an open children's book in his hands and held it up to her as if to say, "Read this to me." She looked down and asked him what he was doing. He replied, "I'm saving you from yourself." She was so shocked that she laughed and her whole mood changed.

## Self-restraint

Another dharmic characteristic is self-restraint. This requires prioritizing the needs and wants of the whole family, including ourselves, and being able to hold back on some wants if they are not in everyone's best interest. Mothering is a wonderful path for self-restraint. One mother said that while driving, she used to yell and curse at other drivers. She called it her way of venting pent-up energy. But once she became a mother and had a small child in the car with her, she saw herself through her child's eyes and stopped doing it.

A real motivation for self-restraint is seeing our children mirror us. Often, we are not even aware of certain ways we act or speak and can be shocked when our children do something offensive, even wondering, "Where did they get that from?"

Noriah had taken her daughter, Larissa, and her friend to the beach. At the end of the day, they were packing up getting ready to go home. Larissa's friend was off in the distance, but Larissa wanted her to come help. In her loudest and sternest voice and with a very fierce look on her face, she yelled out to her friend, "Get over here! Now!" Noriah couldn't believe it. She said, "Larissa, that's a very strong and bossy way to talk to her." Larissa half-smiled and said, "Well, you talk to me like that sometimes, so I thought I'd try it out." Noriah stopped for a minute and thought about what Larissa had just said. Slowly she realized that she did talk to Larissa like that at times when she needed her to do something, and Larissa really wasn't listening. Noriah went on to say that if someone had asked her if she spoke like that, she probably would have honestly said no. But seeing her daughter mirror her put the truth right in her face. "The funny thing is," Noriah ended by saying, "that little smile on her face made me wonder if she didn't do it, consciously or unconsciously, to show me to myself."

Noriah went on to explain that before she was a mother, she was a party person. Life was a playground and fun was what mattered. She didn't take care of herself well at all. "Now as a mother," she says, "if I have to choose between what is fun and what is good for our family life, I choose the latter."

A really close friend was having a barbeque recently and though in some ways, I wanted to go, in other ways I didn't. I knew there'd be a lot of drinking and kids running wild. It's always so hard to get Larissa back to herself after she goes to these events. My husband, Larissa, and I talked about it and in the end, we decided not to go.

Noriah

# SQ: Children's Natural Spiritual Intelligence

Children have access to experiences which are not merely the product of fantasy. Children are capable of levels of perception into what Abraham Maslow called "the farther reaches of human nature."

Thomas Armstrong, *The Radiant Child*

Much of how children teach or guide adults is based on what has come to be known as Spiritual Intelligence (SQ). This is generally referred to as a transcendent quality, recognition of what Tantra Yoga calls The Self or Consciousness. Children are naturally attuned to this quality and draw on it for the intuitive observations and remarks that so often surprise us as adults.

I really see this amazing openness in children. They are much further developed in some ways, can pick up very easily what is happening with peoples' emotions, what is happening around them. It is connecting with the Creator. The way they see, the way they think, it's very intelligent. It is a different kind of logic but it is logic nonetheless.

Eliora

From a very young age, she made this equation in her mind that God equals love. She was very clear about that and that seemed like a reasonable way for a child to frame things. We read a lot and every once in a while, we'd read something that would have spiritual aspects without the dogma and we'd talk about it. With her, I didn't have to teach her anything. Quite the contrary, she came into this world very tapped in.
Marilena


Children are innately high on the intuitional spiritual intelligence spectrum. They quite naturally want the well-being of all respected. Where there are inconsistencies, look out!
Mahima


"Children are always asking, 'Why?' always seeking the meaning of their own and others' actions, always struggling to put feelings and events in a larger, meaningful context," says quantum physicist Danah Zohar. "They want to know who they are, why they were born, where they came from, where the world comes from, and why people behave as they do. When my son was five, he asked me one night at bedtime, 'Mommy, why do I have a life?' That was a spiritually intelligent question."

The beauty of a child's questioning is that it is so elusively simple. Not only is the mother prodded in a split second to think of a direct, uncomplicated, and truthful answer but also she understands that for the child, it is an experiential question and is alive in the moment of being asked. Where an adult may rhetorically and emotionally brood over the question, "Why do I have a life?" a child wants to know it as part of the big picture of being. It is as important as the rain, his friends, how he feels when he plays baseball, his mother's love — all part of weaving the strands of everyday life into an integrated wholeness. While mom's answer may have strengthened his way of inner knowing, his question has the potential of doing the same for her.

> One time we were on a walk when my son was
> a toddler and he was just so happy and said,
> "How did God know how to make everything
> so perfect?"
> Diana

One mother recalls how she and her son, when he was small, always had good conversations during bath time. One time, he looked at her deeply and said, "Mommy, do you know where my ears are?" She laughed. Putting her hands over his ears, she answered, "Right here, on the side of your head, silly!" He giggled and looked at her deeply again. "No," he replied. Taking her hands and placing them over his heart, he told her, "They're right here. You listen with your heart." She understood that at that moment, he was her teacher.

Children sometimes make very spiritually intelligent observations, much wiser sounding than we might do in the same situation. Anandi had such an experience with her five-year-old son, Jesse. He had enjoyed school in the beginning but after some time, one of the boys started bullying others. Not only did he bully, but he slowly gathered a group of boys around him as his gang. Jesse started having a hard time going to school because he didn't know how to handle it. He and his mother talked about it often and together they came up with some ideas. In one of these conversations, there was a lull in talking while Jesse was thinking. Then he said, "It's strange, Mum. The good has become bad and the bad has become good." For a five-year-old, that was quite an insightful comment.

Kristina tells of how astonishingly intuitive her three-year-old daughter, Alessa, was with her yet unborn brother. When Kristina was pregnant for the second time, she did not tell anyone at first, not even Alessa. One day, Alessa came up to her and said, "Mama, you're pregnant." Kristina replied by saying that, yes, they were thinking about becoming pregnant soon. But Alessa only repeated, "No, you're pregnant now." And of course, she was right. Some months later, the doctors wanted Kristina to have an amniocentesis, an exam in which a needle is inserted through the abdomen into the uterus to draw out a sample of amniotic fluid. Kristina was reluctant to do the exam. Despite being nervous about it, finally she agreed. The day of the exam, Kristina and her husband left the house, not telling Alessa where they were going or what was going to be done. They simply said they were going out and Grandma would be with her. When they arrived home later in the day, Alessa jumped up immediately when they came through the door, went up silently to Kristina and without a word, put her hand on Kristina's abdomen, on the exact spot where the needle had been inserted. After a few seconds, she just as silently took her hand away and went back to playing. Kristina was stunned. Once she realized that somehow Alessa intuitively knew what had happened, she was flooded with emotion. "I can only assume that she was giving her brother a soothing, calming touch after his experience," she said. "And most probably, soothing me, as well."

There is a spiritual connection still alive between children and the Consciousness of creation and it may happen that something very vast breaks through into the child's awareness.

Yahaira's daughter, Lana, seemed to have such an opening between worlds one time when they were at a beautiful lake. It was a gorgeous day, very peaceful in the exquisiteness of the tropical forest setting. They were sitting in silence, admiring the water plants that created a kind of green carpet on the surface of the lake, undulating in the soft waves. Suddenly Lana spoke with an immense depth in her voice, "I created this water for these little plants to float on." Yahaira recalls that she looked over at her daughter and saw her focusing intently on the water and the plants, in a very deep mood, as though trying to bring up something from hidden places in her memory. Yahaira asked her, "How did you do that?" After a pause, Lana slowly answered, "I don't know. I don't remember. But I created this water."

The bottom line is that children will express such intelligence when they know they will be heard and understood. Unfortunately, too many parents, as well as educational systems focused almost solely on cognitive development, do not recognize or validate intuitional, spiritual intelligence. If it is not acknowledged and encouraged in children, it may die out after some time, or it may go underground until a more appropriate time in the future. In certain children, some or much of this intelligence may remain, despite not being able to be expressed. But for most, receptive and respectful adults are a valuable encouragement for such awareness to grow. In the process of being open to them, we grow just as much or more.

Chapter 9

# The Yogic Mind: Integration and Transcendence

*The all-round perfect sadhana is the sustained effort to identify every kosa (level of the mind) with the inner self completely.*
P.R. Sarkar, *This World and the Next*

## From Bliss to Body & Back Again

Tantra Yoga understands that the mind holds within itself many dimensions of reality, from the purely physical to the sublimely spiritual. The Sanskrit word used to describe the levels of mind is kosa (or kosha), meaning "the inner self." There are five kosas plus an additional one related to the physical body. The goal is to develop and use every layer of being, to expand the mind's awareness from the mundane to the mystical, from the finite to the infinite. States of being associated with the body, the intellect and emotions, and even extrasensory experiences, are impermanent. When we experience them, we are relating to Consciousness in its outer forms. However — and this is the important point — Pure Consciousness, that which is unaffected by outer layers, is the nucleus, the inner self deep in the core of each level. The task at hand is to use the outer to bring us to the inner.

The kosas are roughly analogous to the conscious, subconscious, and unconscious minds but with a big difference. Western psychology views the self, as noted by quantum physicist Danah Zohar, only as "a combination of unconscious motives, behavioral characteristics, genetic tendencies and neural operations." But in reality, there is something deeper. Zohar describes it as "a permeating center that cannot itself be seen or expressed." It is precisely this center, the Consciousness at the nucleus of each level, which Tantra Yoga understands not only permeates everything in existence but is calling us to Itself. Calling us to recognize that this is what we are.

To realize this center, the incarnating mind needs a physical form as a tool through which to express and refine itself. Without the body, the brain, the nervous system and so on, the mind would have no way to focus itself towards the goal of self-realization. The challenge is not to confuse the tools for the finished product. We are far from being only bodies, brains, thoughts, and feelings. Identifying ourselves with the lower kosas of desires, appearance, health, personality, or intellectual knowledge can lock us into drudgery or inescapable pain. Gradual realization of the higher kosas is what brings beauty into our everyday lives.

There is a Zen saying, "Before enlightenment: chopping wood and carrying water. After enlightenment: chopping wood and carrying water." As long as we are in these physical bodies, we will be carrying out the same tasks every day to take care of ourselves and others. The secret is in how we perceive the world, from what level of awareness we chop wood and carry water, drive our cars, brush our teeth or take care of our children. It is about gradually actualizing all the kosas so as to draw on inner resources from *all* levels of being in our movement towards self-realization. The joy is in each deepening level of awareness becoming sweeter and more sublime.

It's like going on a treasure hunt. Each clue magnetically lures us along until finally we've found and claimed the treasure. By the time that happens, we've gone through so many learning curves and overcome so many obstacles that we laugh at how we missed the obvious truth — the treasure was in the hunt itself and not only at the end of the rainbow. The precious treasure was hidden in full view the whole time.

A note of interest here is that Sarkar's explanation of kosas differs slightly from the traditional Vedanta model. He was a contemporary spiritual master and as such, he understood that the mind has grown in complexity since the ancient yogis first laid this out as a map to the soul. The point remains that the voyage is about moving into ever subtler and subtler realms of being.

In the next sections, we explore some of the ways the inherent drive to realize each kosa manifests between infant and mother. Crucial to this exploration is the need to emphasize, once again, the interdependent partnership of this exchange. On every level, the mother-infant relationship is designed as an exquisite orchestration of coordinated cooperation. Within that context, mama is unquestionably guiding her infant in the gradual awakening of the lower kosas while attempting to keep alive the inspiration of the higher. And her infant is revealing to her, if she lets him, a glimpse into the subtle bliss of the mind's higher realms.

## Physical Body

The starting point is the physical body. According to Sarkar, this is considered an additional kosa as it is the heaviest material layer of life whereas the remaining five layers express the subtler levels of existence.

The physical body provides us with the incomparable service of giving shelter to the incarnating mind. It acts as a superbly designed medium through which we interact with the world around us. How the physical body functions, how it serves us and how we serve it, are paramount as the foundations upon which the passage through this lifetime rests.

The development of this kosa begins in pregnancy, a time of instinctively unobstructed growth for the infant and an expanded sense of physical abilities for the mother. Then comes childbirth, a time of connection with the body as an instrument of extraordinary power and proficiency for both mother and baby. After birth, the infant grows exponentially, unparalleled at any time other time of life, and the mother's body realigns itself with resiliency and adaptability. These periods offer both partners the potential to align with their bodies in unprecedented ways.

It is the remarkable synchronization of the infant's and mother's bodies that lays the groundwork for the maturation of this kosa. The fundamental starting point is that the mother is literally the ground of being for the infant, physically and in every way. Her body continues to regulate the infant much as it did during pregnancy. "Physiologically," says Sue Gerhardt in *Why Love Matters,* "baby is still part of mother's body."

> The baby depends on her for milk, to regulate heart and blood pressure, and to provide immune protection. Muscular activity is regulated by her touch as is growth hormone level. Her body keeps baby warm, and she disperses baby's stress hormones by her touch and her feeding. This basic physiological regulation keeps baby alive.
> Sue Gerhardt, *Why Love Matters*

This can be hard for us as adults to grasp. When a newborn or small infant is hungry, for example, she experiences a sensation that she has no name for, does not know what it is and cannot alleviate on her own. When adults are hungry, we may be uncomfortable, but we know it is from hunger. A baby experiences one sensation after the other all day, only gradually developing a frame of reference within which to cope and make sense of it all. Human infants are the least neurologically mature of any primate, depending totally on biological regulation by mother or caregiver far longer than any other species.

"It's not just the mother changing the infant's … physiological status," says James McKenna, director of the Mother-Baby Behavioral Sleep Laboratory at Notre Dame University. "The infant is regulating the mother's physiological status, as well." The interactions between mother and baby, for example, have a direct effect on the amounts of certain hormones secreted in each of them. How they respond to each other triggers the activation of brain and neurological systems. Touch and closeness help to regulate biological stress mechanisms in them both.

A few of the outstanding means of physiological regulation are: co-sleeping, breastfeeding, and infant massage.

## Co-sleeping

An often-overlooked mechanism of metabolic regulation has to do with baby and mother sleeping together. "Co-sleeping is biologically appropriate and evolved," asserts James McKenna founder of the Mother-Baby Behavioural Sleep laboratory at the University of Notre Dame. "There are thousands of different ways according to the culture." Co-sleeping doesn't refer to a particular method. It relates rather to mother and baby being in close enough proximity, usually described as no more than an arms-length apart, to detect and respond to each other's sensory stimuli such as sound, movement, smell, sight, and so on. It is the immediate sensitivity to the presence of the other that is the particularly crucial factor. The closeness to the mother's body helps regulate baby's temperature, breathing, heart rate, blood pressure, and hormonal status during the night.

## Breastfeeding

Let's take a look at just a few of the innumerable physical benefits of breastfeeding . Mother's milk, including colostrum in the first few days after birth, is without exception the best for baby's digestion and elimination. It's the perfect substance to let the infant's body sink into the most basic, essential metabolic rhythm of taking in, digesting, utilizing, and letting go of waste with a naturalness that can last a lifetime. This may seem obvious but formulas don't prime the infant's body in this same way, potentially resulting in constipation, air gulping and indigestion, fewer natural antibodies and a less than optimum mix of healthy intestinal microorganisms.

Breastmilk is far from a static substance. Rather, its nutritional, hormonal, and immunological qualities change throughout the day and from day to day, according to the individual needs of the infant. "The hormones that help facilitate sleep or waking up are present in the milk," says lactation researcher Katherine Hinde. "Day milk is going to have a completely different hormonal milieu than night milk." Hinde tells us that when the infant's immune system is becoming compromised, the mother's body immediately kicks in to produce the appropriate antibodies which then are passed through her milk. And when the danger has passed, her baby's body lets hers know that those antibodies are no longer needed. In other words, mama's body is always alert and ready to protect her infant.

An additional bonus is that a breastfeeding mother does not have to get up during the night to prepare formula, allowing her to lay down or sit in bed during night feeds. This can help to alleviate the sometimes extreme sleep deprivation that mothering an infant can create.

## Infant Massage

The value of infant massage simply cannot be stressed enough. For a newborn who does not know what her body is or how it functions, massaging embeds in her mind the literal form and shape of the structure she lives within. With loving, repetitive strokes, the mother is conveying, "These are your legs. They support you well. These are your arms. They reach out to the world. This is your body which holds you upright, carries you around, houses your organs and gives a home to your heart and mind. Know it well. Feel good about it. It is a wonderful ally for you in your journey through life."

Physically, the benefits of massage are almost endless. It helps babies to gain weight faster, be more alert, have better digestion and elimination, sleep well, have healthy immune systems, and on and on. Massage literally helps the infant's body to biologically mature. Besides this, loving touch is one of the most primal and powerful means of communicating love between mother and infant. This not only helps the infant to feel more at home in her body, but can cause a surge of relaxing, loving hormones in both mother and baby that decrease stress and prime their systems for calmer, more connected responses to life events.

Infant massage encourages the mother-infant sensory connection. The child and parent smell each other, feel each other. The child hears your singing or speaking, The parent hears the child responding. Sensory communication and bonding uplifts and pleases both.

MJ Glassman, *Neohumanist educator*

Some of these mothering customs may seem to fly in the face of commonly accepted parenting norms and some are making a comeback, but all have been around since mothers began mothering. "Until recent historic periods in the western industrialized world, no human infants were ever separated from their caregivers," says James McKenna. "For the human infant … contact with another body IS love … in the most profound and scientific sense."

Every part of me loves this child and feels loved in return. I feel it in my body, as though my muscles and bones are alive with this love.

Chrisanthi

## Mother's self-care

A mother's physical being undergoes such extraordinarily massive changes during pregnancy, birth, and infancy that she is almost always in a state of flux. Riding those waves can be challenging. She needs good food and ideally, enough rest and support from others to go on with a clear mind. This level requires as much attention as possible from mothers and those around them.

My mom was always with me, and I really needed the help. I was very fragile, very disturbed and could easily get angry. All the time I needed to breastfeed and so many things. I couldn't even take a shower. I was able to care for myself at least a little because of her being around.

Serra

The mother-baby class I attended was really helpful when my daughter was small. We learned what the instructor called yoga "mini-movements," which were really just a stretch here and there but they were simple enough to fit into my day. In fact, doing some of them while I had my baby in a sling was good for her as well.

Alisa

Through breastfeeding, it became so clear to me that my body was like a temple, and I had to take care of it. Almost everything I did and everything I ate became milk for my daughters. It was no longer just my body or just about me.

Lavanya

# The Root or Conscious Mind

The basic, root mind is the first of the subtler kosas and is roughly equivalent to the conscious mind. It contains the instinctive, survival urges as well as the seeds or potential for complete unfolding. The need for food and sleep exists side by side with innate desires for mental expansion, intuition, and longing for the Divine. How those seeds will sprout or not sprout depends on many factors and complex interactions but in all humans, the potential for a full life with deep realization is embedded in the root or base level of awareness.

The development of this kosa hinges on the very basic struggle to survive, grow, and develop ourselves as totally as possible. The driving urge here is a resounding declaration, "I want to live. I want to live fully and well. I want to be and do all that I have come here for." There is almost a ferociousness in the infant's inherent determination to live and thrive. That same ferociousness manifests itself in many mothers as an overpowering drive to love and protect her offspring.

> After she was born and we settled in, the next day I remember thinking that if anyone even considered harming this child, I'd tear them apart. That's how strong this love was.
> Joanna

> The feeling I have for my children is a fierce protection. I feel like a wild wolf or a bear, that I would do whatever it takes to keep them safe, to keep them healthy and on the path. It's a non-compromise zone for me.
> Zoe

Cognitively, for the infant, this level of the mind is buzzing with sensorial input. Earthly life is perceived through the senses and the infant's senses are on high alert all the time. Every sound, every touch, every glance or facial expression, literally every stimulation is used to form the framework for life. An example of how the senses intertwine in small babies is the way they see faces, something they love looking at almost more than anything else. Infant researcher Daniel Stern notes that, "The face makes a unique world" for an infant. The baby may stare intently, for example, at the mouth of the adult holding her, fascinated by these two things (lips) that move, have color and shape, reveal white objects (teeth) and seem to be connected with a sound (adult's voice) which surrounds and envelops the awareness of the infant. This is also why infants instinctively reach their hands to the adult's mouth, to add the sense of touch to the visual and auditory exploration. Or an infant may stare at the adult's hairline, fascinated by the contrast of dark and light. The first kosa of mundane awareness is taking in, all at once, everything seen, felt, or heard as well as smelled and tasted.

Mama's growth and development is on a massive upswing along with her infant's. The focused attention of mothering has the potential to clear out the clutter in this kosa, affording great cause for reflection and ultimately, helping realign everyday priorities.

> Before motherhood, I was free and footloose and did what I wanted. Now if I have to choose between what I want to do and what is best for our family life, I think of the family first. And I feel good about it.
>
> Nalinda

In setting those priorities, the mother's purposeful intentions and life values are important. To maintain clarity of purpose, a mother striving for physical, mental, and spiritual balance aims to be guided by ethics that speak of long-term welfare for all. This may sound like setting a standard of unreachable saintliness for mothers, but it is far from it. One's life perspectives change exponentially through mothering. As that happens, a life based on universal themes of non-harm, respect, cooperation, compassion, seeing the good in everyone, and so on can have a major impact not only on her but potentially on the infant's budding framework of *I want*, *I need*, and *I am*.

Stability and clarity in this kosa are greatly affected by pregnancy and birth. Upon entering this life, the initial task for an infant is to truly enter it, mentally and emotionally as well as physically. The same is true for the mother upon entering motherhood. The safe and loving passage from the womb to the world is a fundamental prerequisite for both infant and mother to feel at home in their bodies and minds. Traumatic events during birth, all too often unrecognized as traumatic by mothers and birth attendants alike, can cause a disassociation from the body and the surroundings in both mother and baby. Overly clinical, medical approaches to birth may create fear, isolation, mental/emotional paralysis, a disturbance of the innate magnetism between mother and baby and a myriad of other symptoms that affect some babies and mothers for years to come.

But whether pregnancy and birth were joyous or traumatic (or a combination of both), settling into the reality of this new life can be greatly benefited by mothering practices accentuating closeness between her and her infant. Breastfeeding, co-sleeping, and infant massage, mentioned in the physical body kosa as helping to regulate the physiological functioning of the body, are important in this kosa for helping the infant's mind to enter the body fully and the mother's mind to clearly reorganize itself in the configuration needed for the mothering years ahead.

Of all the intentions embedded in this kosa, that of spiritual longing is the deepest of human yearnings. By following this urge in whatever ways resonate within her, a mother is indirectly acknowledging, responding to and accentuating the infant's innate spiritual nature, hopefully giving it a nudge to stay alive well into the baby's future life.

# The Intellectual, Emotional or Subconscious Mind

Deeper than the root mind is the layer of thoughts, memory, emotions, and the experience of pleasure and pain. Perhaps most importantly, it is where experiences morph into our own unique philosophy of life, one which has an enormous subconscious effect on how our lives unfold.

Here we have the means of making sense of what we perceive from the outside world. Though deeper kinds of cognitive function take all the years of childhood to develop, infants are well aware of their world and filing away every bit of information for later use. The sensory images of the face put together by the infant in the first kosa get imbued with nuance in this layer. The infant *feels* the feelings behind the facial gestures. He does not intellectually understand the feelings, but they are nonetheless stored away in the deeper, preverbal levels of awareness. Because the rational higher brain is largely underdeveloped in infants, they are creatures of absorption rather than discernment. They don't screen out an event or a tone of voice or a gesture as being relevant or irrelevant, good or bad, wanted or unwanted. Everything has impact.

Tantra Yoga tells us that, "Human beings do not forget anything. Everything is imprinted in their minds." This kosa is the repository of memory: both memories of conscious recall as well as those embedded in the below-conscious-awareness memory. Subconscious memories so powerfully mold our perception of life due, to a great extent, to the emotions sensed in this kosa. It is here that unresolved birth or other early trauma may manifest later in life as withdrawal or indifference, lack of confidence, helplessness, or overindulgence leading to addictions. It is just as true, however, that grounded, loving interactions and the right opportunities may develop this kosa as a rich intellect imbued with heartfelt sentiments.

In terms of interaction, infants in the first few months of life are awake but not quite awake. Somewhere around two months, the baby begins to consciously and deliberately interact. She initiates "conversation" by her smiles, looks, and movements, trying to bring about a smile or pleasurable feeling in others. This is the beginning of very real interpersonal skills which flourish when a baby's attempts are responded to. It's also when she begins to feel lost as to how to act when they are not. It is in this level that a mother's responsiveness to her baby's cues begin to create a sense of trust or mistrust in the infant, reinforcing or negating the sense that the world is a place where her needs will be met.

> I couldn't force my will on them when they were tiny. If they were hungry, I breastfed them. If they cried, I picked them up. If they didn't want to sleep, I held them. I tried to be responsive to their needs in a deeply empathetic way.
> Zelda

At the same time, this kind of responsiveness creates a deeper sense of trust for a mother in herself, her instincts, and her intuition. The infant's smiles, the looks, the body gestures, and the heart feeling all combine to help mother understand that no matter what condition the house is in or how much sleep she is missing, she is doing something right. Her baby loves her no matter what. "She can then feel not like 'any mother' but like her child's 'particular mother'," observes author Naomi Stadlen. The world becomes more of a safe and trusting place for everyone involved.

> I was so anxious with my first child about whether I was doing things right. It created a lot of frustration. Now I am more relaxed, and it is much better. In the beginning I didn't feel good

> about all the mistakes I was making. But now,
> it's different. You make mistakes and learn from
> them. I trust myself more.
> Thelma

The nature of the constantly thinking/feeling mind in this kosa can be quieted or redirected somewhat through awareness of one's breath. Everyone knows how breathing speeds up or becomes shallow under the influence of sudden fear or crisis situations and how good it feels to breathe again normally when the immediate crisis has passed. When the stressors for both mothers and babies seem overwhelming, which they often do, the mother's attention to her breathing, using it to calm her mind can have a calming influence on baby as well. A simple technique can be counting 1,2,3 on the inhale and exhale, with even longer exhalations if possible. Additionally, mentally matching the rhythm of the breath with an affirmation such as "love is everywhere" can be a powerful boost to the mind, helping to bring it back to balance.

A note to mention here is about yogic practices of breathing, called pranayama. Generally speaking, these are strong and effective tools for breath awareness but need to be taught by trained teachers. The breath, like any other powerful force in life, can cause as much harm as good if not used properly.

Most infants, starting in pregnancy, spend most of their time processing information related to developing the body and the first two kosas of the mind. At this point in our evolution, a great majority of children and adults everywhere spend most of their lives locked into these lower kosas. Either we barely visit anything higher or if we do, it tends to seem not as important as what we look like, what we have, what we know or how we feel. In fact, most research about infants is related to these kosas and especially to this "thinking" kosa.

But these kosas alone aren't able to give the fullness and richness that life deserves. It is the influence of the third to fifth levels, collectively called the unconscious mind, which truly open the heart and mind, giving depth and purpose to the understandings of the first layers.

## The Supramental Unconscious Mind

The complexity of the unconscious mind incorporates not one but three layers. The supramental layer connects us to beauty, refinement, creative urges, spontaneous insights, certain psychic phenomena, and the sprouting of intuition. When awareness moves beyond the two lower kosas, artistic inspiration, personal insights, and the desire for spiritual realization may emerge from here.

The lower kosas are constantly pulling us towards the external world or our internal chatter. In this kosa, the brain waves begin to slow down and perception moves inward. While the ability to think is in the previous level, the more advanced capacity of self-reflection is in this layer. While auditory and visual skills are alive and functioning from the lowest levels, losing oneself in aesthetic beauty arises from this layer and the next higher as well. One mother noted that having a baby awakened a latent sense of artistic creativity in her, a clear example of this layer of the mind expanding. While a desire for stillness in the seemingly never-ending chaos of daily life may be a thought in the lower kosas, it is in this kosa that the skill is learned. In fact, while giving birth, it is the capability of withdrawing awareness to a deeper and quieter place which many mothers describe as the starting point for falling into a 'birthing mind'.

Babies are active in this kosa. They are intuitive, creative and playful. The small child's obvious sense of wonder, awe, and magic are expressions of this and the next higher kosa. And the intuitive communication between mother and baby begins at this level of the mind.

An integral function of this kosa is opening the door to the incomparable effects of music. The Sufi saying, "The infant is music itself" expresses the innateness of rhythm and sound that babies come hardwired with. They seem to really listen, sometimes moving as though dancing. Infants are often soothed or quieted by restful, familiar music, especially music they heard while in the womb. Besides just listening to music, infants love to be sung to. Because they may not yet understand the actual words, it is the way of expression, the emotional subtlety, and the sincerity of the song and the singer that matters the most. What they sense under the words and sounds becomes for them the transmission of almost totally heartfelt feeling, a powerful means of conveying intention to very deep levels of their being.

The yogic chant, *Baba Nam Kevalam*, is a particularly soothing, resonant, and meaningful mantra to sing or listen to, for infants and mothers alike. It means that all of existence is the expression of one Infinite Consciousness and that cultivating our uniquely personal relationship with that Consciousness is why we are here. The vastness and scope of the word *Baba* implies something that our intellects cannot understand, an unfathomable love that our souls know very well and long to be in union with. Because this universal mantra is sung to hundreds of different melodies, mothers can find ones they like and when they tire of a tune, there are scores of others to choose a new favorite from. After a while, the mind is effortlessly hearing this mantra throughout the day, allowing its truth to seep into every aspect of life.

This kosa, then, begins to tap into realms of awareness beyond the mental and emotional. Though mother and infant are always guiding and helping each other, in the lower kosas the mother is stronger. But from this kosa onwards, the baby may be the one to guide the mother. She may be learning from him, especially if she is aware of the depth of his message. These are the kosas of the heart and transcendence, areas in which babies may outshine adults.

## The Subliminal Unconscious Mind

Awareness in this level brings us in touch with the inspiration of the soul, insights into true knowledge, wisdom, hope, love, and forgiveness. This kosa and the next are most notably the places of bliss from where the infant's mind radiates its particularly special qualities. This kosa is related to the heart and an infant's heart is wide open.

In this level, mothers' and babies' intuitive communication really flourishes. Mothers instinctively speak in low, soft tones to their babies, in the intimate way of lovers. It has been said that when people are angry, they shout because the anger has created a distance between their hearts. The angrier they are, the louder they will shout to try to cross that chasm. But when people feel love, they talk softly. The distance between their hearts is very small. The distance between mother and child is designed to be very, very small indeed.

> I realized after she was some months old how often I understood what she needed. It amazed me, really. I might have to try different ways to respond to her, especially if I was tired or overwhelmed. But when my mind and heart were clear, I just somehow knew. And now, even though she can speak, I still know so often without words what she needs or is thinking.
> Nellie

It is not by accident that mothers (and other adults) tend to carry babies on the left against their chests. Clare Porac, professor of psychology at Pennsylvania State University, notes that this "cradling bias" is a universal behavior shown around the world, especially in early infancy, and is even seen in primates like chimpanzees. Theories abound as to the reasons for this, but closeness to the mother's heart is undoubtedly significant, perhaps physiologically and energetically having a soothing effect on both baby and caregiver.

It is in this kosa that women in labor will take the withdrawal of the senses experienced in the previous kosa and concentratedly focus on that which allows the baby and the body to birth as they know how to do. Mother after mother speaks about moving beyond fear and control by surrendering and concentrating on sinking into the contractions rather than the pain, fear or desire to control.

The two main characteristics of this kosa are the qualities of conscience and non-attachment. It is here that we can clearly differentiate between what is good for us and others and what isn't. On top of that, we gain the ability to say no to those influences that bring our minds down and walk away from them without regret.

> I was very wild and out-of-control in my 20s. But somehow having the children brought me into alignment with myself and with the universal life force. It's been a very powerful experience for me.
> Ziina

This kosa is also the seat of samskaras, or reactions to actions. Thoughts and actions, whether good or bad, create corresponding reactions which we carry with us in our disembodied mind from lifetime to lifetime. What this means is that the samskaras we are born with determine factors beyond our control. It is samskara, not random coincidence, that our parents, siblings, and significant others are who they are. Each mother is the perfect mother for all of her children and vice versa. Whether relationships and life circumstances are painful or pleasurable, they are always meant to be used to bring us closer to our truth.

This level brings an emerging and profound resonance with the truth of *Consciousness as Love* and lets us see more clearly the limitations of the passing reality in everyday life. Our hearts truly soar with the touch of the Divine. In one way, this confers more beauty to the passing world. In another way, it pulls us out of the external forms of the world into the heart of creation, where we connect to and long for only the experience of its inner essence.

## The Golden Kosa: Pure Unconscious Mind

The last level of the causal mind is called the golden kosa. In this place of being, one experiences all of creation and all of life as One. When we said earlier that infants live within the universal rhythm, that they feel no separation from all of life, it is the influence of this kosa and awareness beyond the kosas. When small children sense that flowers or stones are alive, it is not an intellectual thought. They feel the oneness on a very real, experiential level.

In this kosa, the sound and essence of love occupy one's interior being to the point that one lives bliss, becomes bliss. This is the absolutely subtlest awareness of *I* where there is only *I am*.

The *Atman* or soul, however, exists higher than any of the levels of mind. The only longing left in the *I* of the golden kosa is to become one with the bliss of the *I-less* soul. Like a river merging into the vastness of the ocean, we find the true expansiveness of who we are. We have become Love itself ... what more could anyone want?

> What I cry out for, like every being, with my whole life and all my earthly passion, is ... to lose oneself in the unfathomable, to plunge into the inexhaustible, to be absorbed in immensity... and to give of one's deepest to that whose depth has no end.
> Pierre Teillhard de Chardin, *On Love and Happiness*

Every infant comes into life with this longing. So did we as infants. This longing still exists within us. It is not an exaggeration to say that the mother-infant partnership may be more valuable than we realize in propelling us towards fulfilling this longing.

Chapter 10

# Love: The Driving Force of Evolution

*The most telling and profound way of describing the evolution of the universe would undoubtedly be to trace the evolution of love.*

Pierre Teilhard de Chardin, *On Love and Happiness*

## A Thumbnail Look at Science, Love, Spirituality, & Evolution

Western science has turned its probing eyes and expanding heart towards the biology of love, spirituality, and evolution and is casting light on their convergence. David Loye, a prominent researcher on Darwin's *Other Theory*, is explicit that Darwin emphasized love, care, and cooperation as stronger catalysts for evolution than the "survival of the fittest."

> ... though we are selfish, we are also driven by love to transcend selfishness and ... though fiercely motivated to survive and prevail, we are also driven by the transcendent need to respect and care for the needs of others ...The more

important elements for us are love and the distinct emotion of sympathy.

David Loye, *Prologue: The Truth About Darwin – and Us*

Loye discovered that Darwin wrote extensively of the evolution-shaping power of mutual aid, love, education, even religion, and above all, of the power of the moral sense: i.e., an evolutionary inbuilt moral imperative for doing right rather than wrong to others. Cellular biologist Bruce Lipton concurs by noting that, "New evolution insights are telling us that evolution isn't competition. Evolution is based on cooperation. We are individuals but we are interdependent with the whole. All humans are working as one living system."

The outdated concept of evolution as a dog-eat-dog phenomenon may gradually be being replaced with a futuristic view of cooperation and love as more important catalysts. Chilean biologist Humberto Maturana is convinced that love is inherently biological and linked evolutionarily with our ever-increasing intelligence.

> We are not talking about love as a virtue or as something good from a moral, religious, or philosophical perspective. We are talking biology, we are talking about our animal constitution as the particular kind of primates that we are, as members of an evolutionary trend centered around ... the biology of love and the expansion of intelligence. Love is the grounding of our existence as humans.
>
> Humberto Maturano, *Biology of Love*

Spanish biologist Enrique Burunat sees love's implications as being pivotal in the emerging description of humankind's origins. "Love, once considered as merely a simple emotion," he writes, "(is) at the very core of explaining the evolutionary characteristics of the human being." His extensive research points to love, with an emphasis on maternal love, as the biological motivation behind the development of language, brain development, the emergence of the "social brain" and corresponding social structures, and in short, for the main features of humanity. "The human species," he asserts, "would not have arisen without the creation of love by natural selection."

Taking this all a step further are the scientists defining love in terms of spirituality and transcendence. Love, as a force spiritual in nature, pulls us towards an ever-increasing awareness of what spirituality is. Neuroscientists Beauregard and O'Leary state that "the spiritualization of consciousness is indeed a trend in human evolution" while years of research in the field of neurotheology points to brain structures and neural pathways explicitly committed to mysticism, transcendence, and identification with something far larger than ourselves. "Once we recognize that spirituality has a biological basis, we realize that we must have evolved towards spirituality," writes George Vaillant, professor at Harvard Medical School. "Love is the shortest definition of spirituality."

## Tantric Evolution & the Attraction of Cosmic Love

> Each and every living being has got the longing
> for the Great.
> P.R. Sarkar, *Longing for the Great*

As impactful as mother-child and all other forms of human love are in our evolutionary journey, Tantra Yoga recognizes that the major evolutionary force is a love far greater than any human love could possibly be. Tantric cosmology speaks of evolution as the process by which Consciousness allows life to emerge from Itself while, at the same time, creating the means to bring that life back to Itself. The cycle begins with the subtlest, highest, unexpressed Consciousness gradually metamorphosing Itself into more and more densified elements – vibrational waves, ether, air, light, liquid, and finally, solid matter. In this, the outward phase of creation, Consciousness hides itself in heavier and heavier created forms.

Having arrived at the zenith of density in matter, Consciousness then begins the inward movement of pulling creation back to its pure form. It emerges from matter as a very rudimentary mind, starting out in the simplest of animate beings. The newly formed mind becomes gradually more expanded as it passes through higher life forms, eventually evolving into the human mind. Humans are the only expressions of Consciousness with a self-reflective awareness. Thus, we are the only ones with the capacity to direct our thoughts and potentialities towards the completion of life's journey, that is, transcendence and merger once again with pure, unmanifested Being. The odyssey of existence is that of Consciousness emanating from and ultimately returning to Itself.

> (From Consciousness to the inanimate and ...) From the inanimate to the animate goes the process of evolution. Consider a piece of stone, for instance. It has neither the power of action nor the sensation of mind. What is the reason? It is because hitherto there has been no manifestation of mind in the stone. Consider the trees and plants that are more animate than the stone. There is activity in them. They grow, draw the vital juice from the earth, maintain

their species by creating seeds in their own bodies, and enjoy and suffer pleasure and pain when taken care of or hurt. We see in them the manifestation of consciousness, for mind has awakened in them. Thus, progressing on the path of mental development, we see in humanity its greatest manifestation. Just as evolution takes place from the subtle to the crude, similarly the unit entity reverts step by step from the crude to the subtle, towards the same Absolute Consciousness from whence it came. It is just like the waves of the sea, rippling back from whence they have come.

P.R. Sarkar, *Evolution Towards Perfection*

Consciousness then, as both the source and the goal of life, is the stuff of existence, the nucleus of all created entities. The inexpressible vastness of created forms are but variations on a theme: Consciousness mutating Itself into this fish or that tree, these humans or those galaxies and nebulae. As Sarkar says, "All molecules, atoms, electrons, protons, positrons and neutrons are the veritable expressions of the same Supreme Consciousness."

This implies that though outward expressions vary, the inner identity of everything is the same. Following on the heels of that thought comes the inescapable realization of the utter interconnectedness of all that exists. Another name for Consciousness is Love, that which binds or connects all that is. It is the realization of this Love that we are evolving towards. As a species, we fleetingly catch glimpses of it now and then only to return to our state of normalcy within which we see ourselves as separate from everything else.

Tantra Yoga recognizes that the attraction of the Great, the pull of an Absolute Primordial Consciousness calling us home, is the strongest force in evolution. This does not at all discredit the physical, mental, and material evolutionary causes propounded by the natural sciences. It only adds a depth that has been missing. Goaded on by the desire for fulfillment that will never be satiated by people, places, objects, feelings, or ideas, spiritual urges take their place not only amongst the forces of evolution but indeed, at its very core.

## Mother-Child Love & Evolution: Where Is It Going?

The universal love which has remained suppressed in the human mind is bound to express itself one day. That day is not very far away.
P.R. Sarkar, *The True Nature of Bhakti*

The planet needs the care and cooperation that mothers and children represent. The intuitive mothering model, by the very nature of its heart, moves side by side with men and fathers realizing that they, and we, are each integral parts of the picture. It embraces children as whole beings who are extraordinary teachers of heart qualities. It understands the fertile power of technology, science, and cultural expressions when they are based on an ethic of welfare for all. It pulsates with the irrefutable truth that women everywhere must come forward as powerful agents for social change. Women as mothers have the potential to mother all of life as their own family.

What's more, the consciousness of the planet may be ready for this mothering in ways that it never was before. The current planetary unsustainability is registering itself in the collective mind as a reality. Sustainability, on all levels, is what mothers are good at. The continuation and evolution of the species has always depended on the sustaining quality of mothering that has for so long gone unnoticed but not lost.

The collective consciousness of mother-child love, which women have carried within from the beginning of human history, is biologically primed to spur on the evolution of love. As mother-infant love played a remarkably crucial role in our evolution up until now, so it is continuing to be a blueprint for the next jump to universality.

> Let women be the vanguard of a new revolution (i.e., a transformative change in collective consciousness) which humanity must achieve for a glorious tomorrow.
> P.R. Sarkar, *Women's Rights*

# Sources

**Preface**
- Sarkar, P.R. "Trio in Spiritual Progress," *Subhasita Samgraha 12,* Electronic Edition 9: the Works of P.R. Sarkar, 2018.

**Ch 1 Mother-Infant Love**

*Partnership and Promise*
- St Therese of Liseux. "Therese on Love." https://www.pathsoflove.com/love-therese.html.
- Sarkar, P.R. "Cooperatives." *Proutist Economics.* Calcutta: Ananda Marga Publications, 1992, 129.
- Sarkar, P.R. "Individual Rhythm and Universal Rhythm." *Ananda Marga Philosophy in a Nutshell Part 4,* Calcutta: Ananda Marga Publications.

*Mother-Child Love and Evolution: Where It All Began*
- Lampert, Ada. *The Evolution of Love,* Connecticut: Praeger Publishers, 1997,17.
- Dalton, Rex. "Little Lucy fossil found." *Nature Magazine,* 20 September 2006.
- National Geographic. "Foot of 'World's Oldest Child' Shows How Our Ancestors Moved."
- https://www.nationalgeographic.com/science/article/australopithecus-afarensis-lucy-selam-dikika-paleontology.
- PBS Nova. *Becoming Human — First Steps.* https://www.pbs.org/wgbh/nova/video/becoming-human-part-1/.
- Meek, Leslie. University of Minnesota. http://cda.morris.umn.edu/~meeklesr/love.html.
- Allot, Robin. "Evolutionary Aspects of Love and Empathy." *Journal of Social and Evolutionary Systems,* Volume 15 Number 4. 353-370, 1992.
- Lampert, Ada. *ibid,* 116.

### *The Bigger Picture: Universal Love and Social Change*

- Sarkar, P.R. "Neohumanism is the Ultimate Shelter." *Liberation of the Intellect,* Electronic Edition 9: the Works of P.R. Sarkar, 2018.
- Sarkar, P.R. "Devotional Sentiment and Neohumanism." *The Liberation of Intellect: Neohumanism,* Calcutta: Ananda Marga Publications, 1982, 7.
- Williams, Kyodo. "Complete Interview Angel Kyodo Williams," *The Global Oneness Project,* Feb. 25, 2009.
- Sarkar, P.R. "Mundane and Transcendental Love." *Discourses on Neohumanist Education* Ananda Marga Publications, 1998, 63.
- Bussey, Marcus. *Gurukul Webinar "Evolution of Consciousness: A Neohumanist Story."* Feb. 22, 2014. http://gurukul.edu/resourcesx/webinars-archive/.
- Eisler, Riane. "The Way of Partnership." from *The Goddess Shift* by Stephanie Marohn
- California: Elite books, 2010), 15.
- Sarkar, P.R. "The Spirit of Society." *PROUT in a Nutshell Vol 2, Part 9,* Electronic Edition 9: the Works of P.R. Sarkar, 2018.
- Sarkar, P.R. "Social Discourses." *The Thoughts of P.R. Sarkar* Electronic Edition 9: the Works of P.R. Sarkar, 2018.
- Beauregard, Maurice and Denyse O'Leary. *The Spiritual Brain: A Neuroscientist's Case for the Existence of the Soul.* Canada: Harper Collins,2007, 294-295.

### *Tantra Yoga in a (Very Small) Nutshell*

- Sarkar, P.R. "Tantra and Its Effects on Society." *Discourses on Tantra Vol 2,* Calcutta: Ananda Marga Publications, 1994), 24.
- Sarkar, P.R. *Ibid.*
- Sarkar, P.R. "Vrajagopála and Aesthetic Science." *Namami Krsnasundaram,* Ananda Marga Publications, 1981, 214.

## Ch 2 Infant Love

### *The Infant's Enigmatic Mind: Spacious and Sweet*

- Chamberlain, David. *Mind of Your Newborn Baby.* California: North Atlantic Books, 1998, 193.
- Armstrong, Thomas. "The Spiritual Origins of Childhood." *Sunrise Magazine,* October/November 1984. Copyright © 1984 by Theosophical University Press. Excerpted from *Mothering magazine,* Summer 1984.
- Wright, Jody. *Parenting from the Heart* Mass: Motherwear Inc, 1996, 83.

- Sarkar, P.R. "Individual Rhythm and Universal Rhythm." *Ananda Marga Philosophy in a Nutshell*, Part 4, Electronic Edition 9: the Works of P.R. Sarkar, 2018.
- Sarkar, P.R. "The Means to Save Oneself from Sorrow." *Ananda Vacanamrtam Part 9*. Electronic Edition 9: the Works of P.R. Sarkar, 2018.
- Gopnik, Alison. *Philosophical Baby: What Children's Minds Tell Us About Truth, Love and the Meaning of Life*. New York: Farrar, Strauss and Giroux, 2009, 129, 238-241.

### Infants: A Lot of Love in a Little Body
- Stadlen, Naomi. *How Mothers Love and How Relationships Are Born*. London: Hachette Digital, 2011), 1.
- Gopnik, Alison. *Philosophical Baby: What Children's Minds Tell Us About Truth, Love and the Meaning of Life*. New York: Farrar, Strauss and Giroux, 2009, 175-176.
- Leach, Penelope. *Baby and Child*. London: Penguin, Harmondsworth, 1979, 21, 34, 122 quoted in Robin Allott, "Evolutionary Aspects of Love and Empathy"
- , Journal of Social and Evolutionary Systems, Vol 15 No 4 353-370, 1992
- Stadlen, Naomi. *What Mothers Do Especially When It Looks Like Nothing*. New York: Penguin Books, 2004, 200.
- Didi Ananda Uttama, *Refugee mothers speaking* from the work of AMURTEL Greece https://greece.amurtel.org

### Conversations With Babies: The Art of Listening
- McClure, Vimala. *Path of Parenting: Twelve Principles to Guide Your Journey*. Novato, Calif.: New World Library, 1999, 34.
- McClure, Ibid, 33.
- McClure, Vimala. *Parenting from the Heart*. Mass: Motherwear Inc, 1996, 9-10.
- McClure, Vimala. *Path of Parenting: Twelve Principles to Guide Your Journey*. Novato, Calif: New World Library, 1999, 34.

### Conversations With Babies: The Art of Responding
- Brous, Kathy. *Allan Schore: What Is the Self?* https://attachmentdisorderhealing.com/allan-schore. accessed 05/16/2014.
- Condon, William S. and Louis W. Sander. "Synchrony Demonstrated between Movements of the Neonate and Adult Speech," *Child Development* 45, no. 2, 1974, 456–62. https://doi.org/10.2307/1127968.
- Fine, Jeffrey L. & Dalit Fine, *The Art of Conscious Parenting*. Vermont: Healing Arts Press, 2009, 55-56.
- "Engagement and disengagement.". *The Annual of Psychoanalysis*, edited by the Chicago Institute for Psychoanalysis, Vol XX, N.J.: Analytic Press, 1992, 29.

- Schore, Dr. Allan. "Effects of Secure Attachment Relationship on Right Brain Development, Affect Regulation and Infant Mental Health" quoting Sander 1988. *Infant Mental Health Journal, Vol 22*, 2001.

**Stress and Balance: It All Depends on Joy**
- Sarkar, P.R. "The Practice of Art and Literature." *Discourses on Neohumanist Education*, Calcutta: Ananda Marga Publications, 1998, 76.
- Schore, Dr. Allan. *Affect Dysregulation and Disorders of the Self.* New York: Norton and Co., 2003, 275.
- Sunderland, Margot. *The Science of Parenting*. New York: Penguin Random House, 2006, 90.
- Gerhardt, Sue. *Why Love Matters: How Affection Shapes a Baby's Brain.* London: Routledge, 2009), 22-23.
- Schore, Dr. Allan. "Effects of Secure Attachment Relationship on Right Brain Development, Affect Regulation and Infant Mental Health.*"Infant Mental Health Journal, Vol 22(1-2), 2001.
- Brous, Kathy. *Allan Schore: What Is the Self?* https://attachmentdisorderhealing.com/allan-schore. accessed 05/16/2014.

**The Ultimate Joy: A Larger-Than-life Love**
- Sarkar, P.R. "Shivopadesha 1." *Namah Shivaya Shantaya*, Electronic Edition 9: the Works of P.R. Sarkar, 2018.

## Ch 3 Mother Love

**Mother Love: A Unique Phenomenon**
- Stadlen, Naomi. *What Mothers Do Especially When It Looks Like Nothing*. New York: Penguin Books, 2004, 14.
- Milojevic, Ivana. *Personal correspondence with author.*
- Roy, Denise. *Momfulness*. Calif: Jossey-Bass, 2007, 1.
- Kuchinskas, Susan. *The Chemistry of Connection*. Calif: New Harbinger Publications, 2009), 3, 17.
- Stadlen, Naomi. *How Mothers Love and How Relationships Are Born.* London: Hachette Digital, 2011, 2.
- Fromm, Eric. *The Art of Loving.* New York: Harper & Row, 2006, 5.

**Mother Love and Spirituality: What's the Connection?**
- Hall, Jennifer. Midwifery, Mind and Spirit. Oxford: Elsevier Ltd., 2001.
- Lim, Robin. *Ibu Robin Lim.* https://iburobin.com.
- Zohar, Danah. *Quantum Self.* London: Bloomsbury Publishing, 1990), 133-134.
- Napthali, Sarah. *Buddhism for Mothers.* Australia: Inspired Living, NSW, 2003, 6-7.

### Mother Love: A Stepping Stone to Divine Love
- The Commission for Children at Risk. *"Hardwired to Connect: The New Scientific Case for Authoritative Communities"* sponsored by the Institute for American Values, YMCA of the USA, and Dartmouth Medical School, 2003.
- Thompson, Ross A. and Brandy Randall. "Children's Spiritual Development" from Implementing the UN Convention of the Rights of the Child: A standard of living for development, edited by Arlene Andrews and Natalie Kaufman, http://www.desmos.info/en/doc/Childrens_Spiritual_Development.pdf.
- Zak, Paul J. *Love, Belief and Neurobiology.* Loma Linda video, researchchannel.org.
- Newberg, Andrew. "How God Changes Your Brain: An Introduction to Jewish Neurotheology." *CCAR Journal: The Reform Jewish Quarterly* (Winter 2016), 23.
- Baylor Institute for Studies of Religion. "American Piety in the 21st Century: New Insights to the Depth and Complexity of Religion in the US." *Baylor Religion Survey*, Baylor University, September 2006, 25.
- Hall, T.W. *The Spiritual Transformation Inventory: Spiritual Assessment and the Relational Revolution.* HallCAPPL.ppts (March 2006). Invited presentation to the International Forum on Christian Higher Education, Coalition of Christian Colleges and Universities, Dallas.

### Mothers and Dharma: Motherhood's Ultimate Purpose
- McClure, Vimala. *Path of Parenting: Twelve Principles to Guide Your Journey.* New World Library, Novato, CA, 1999, 1.
- Sarkar, P.R. "The Call of the Supreme.," *SubhásitaSubhásita Samgraha, Part 1,* Electronic Edition 9: the Works of P.R. Sarkar, 2018.
- Sarkar, P.R. "Dharma Sadhana." *Ananda Vacanamrtam 31,* Electronic Edition 9: the Works of P.R. Sarkar, 2018.
- Inayat Khan, Hazrat. "The Education of the Infant." *The Sufi Message of Hazrat Inayat Khan,* Vol. 3, ch 1.
- Sarkar, P.R. *About Madalasa*, "The Place of Women in the Spiritual World." *Awakening of Women,* Calcutta: Ananda Marga Publications, 1995, 171.

### Dharma Unfolded
- Sarkar, P.R. "Dharma Sadhana." *Ananda Vacanamrtam 31,* Electronic Edition 9: the Works of P.R. Sarkar, 2018.
- Interview with Jaak Panksepp, author of *Affective Neuroscience, Foundations of Human and Animal Emotions.* Oxford University Press, NY, 1998, *Brain Science podcast* #65, 1/13/2010.

- Sarkar, P.R. "Where There Is Dharma There Is Ista, and Where There Is Ista There Is Victory." *Subhásita Samgraha Part 12,* Electronic Edition 9: the Works of P.R. Sarkar, 2018.
- Towsey, Michael. *Eternal Dance of Macrocosm.* Copenhagen: Proutist Publications, 1986), 98-100.
- Sarkar, P.R. ." Shivokti 11. " Namah Shivaya Shantaya, Electronic Edition 9: the Works of P.R. Sarkar, 2018.

### *Community Calls*
- Some, Sobonfu. *The Spirit of Intimacy.* New York: Harper-Collins, 2000, 36.
- "New Mothers Speak Out." results of a survey conducted by Childbirth Connection in partnership with Lamaze International, August 2008, 34.
- Volkman, Alisa and Rufus Griscom. "Let's Talk Parenting Taboos." TED talk, Dec. 2010, quoting survey by Mom Central Consulting, 2009.
- Some, Sobonfu. *ibid*, 44-45.
- Interview of Bella DePaulo and Robert Milardo. "Beyond the Nuclear Family." *Vision Magazine,* Summer 2011, http://www.vision.org/visionmedia/extended-family-relationships/47372.aspx
- Simms, Eva. *The Child in the World: Embodiment, Time and Language in Early Childhood.* Detroit: Wayne State University Press, 2008, 17.
- Hrdy, Sarah Blaffer. "Mothers and Others." *Natural History Magazine,* May 2001. https://www.naturalhistorymag.com/picks-from-the-past/11440/mothers-and-others
- "How Moms Socialize Online." *Mom Central Consulting 2009 Survey implications,* http://www.slideshare.net/thopeross/how-moms-socialize-online-implications-for-brands

### *Emotionality and the Kaeshik Sentiment*
- Sarkar, P.R. "Sentimentality: A Special Quality in Women." Excerpt from *The Awakening of Women,* Calcutta: Ananda Marga Publications, 1995), 228.
- Goudreau, Jenna. "The Ten Worst Stereotypes About Powerful Women." *Forbes Magazine,* 10/24/2011. http://www.forbes.com/sites/jennagoudreau/2011/10/24/worst-stereotypes-powerful-women-christine-lagarde-hillary-clinton/
- Sarkar, P.R. *ibid,* 228.
- Lampert, Ada. *Evolution of Love.* Westport, Conn.: Praeger Publishers, 1997, 21.
- Brizendine, Louann. *The Female Brain.* New York: Broadway Books, 2006), 15-18.
- Weinberg, Tronick, Cohn and Olson. "Gender Differences in Emotional Expressivity and Self-Regulation in Early Infancy." *Developmental Psychology,* February 1999, Vol 35, No. 1, 175-188,

- Leeb, Rebecca T. and F. Gillian Rejskind. "Here's Looking at You, Kid! A Longitudinal Study of Perceived Gender Differences in Mutual Gazing Behavior in Young Infants." *Sex Roles*, Vol 50, Nos1/2, January 2004.
- Baron-Cohen, Simon. *The Essential Difference: Men, Women and the Extreme Male Brain*. New York: Penguin Books, 2003.
- Newberg, Andrew & Mark Robert Waldman. *How God Changes Your Brain*. New York: Ballantine Books, 2010.
- Sarkar, P.R. *ibid*, 227.
- Damasio. Antonio. *Descartes' Error: Emotion, Reason and The Human Brain*. New York: Harper Collins, 1994, 128 & 245.
- Zohar, Danah. *Spiritual Intelligence: The Ultimate Intelligence*. London: Bloomsbury Publishing, 2000, 6-7.

### *Devotional Sentiment: The Greatest Treasure of Humanity*

- Sarkar, P.R. "Astitva and Shivatva." The Thoughts of P.R. Sarkar, Electronic Edition 9: the Works of P.R. Sarkar, 2018.
- Jalāl ad-Dīn Muhammad Rūmī. *Look at Love*. translated by Nader Khalili, http://allspirit.co.uk/rumi4.html
- Sarkar, P.R. "Devotional Sentiment and NeoHumanism." *The Liberation of Intellect: Neohumanism*. Electronic Edition 9: the Works of P.R. Sarkar, 2018.

### Ch 4 Mothers and Meditation: The Challenge and the Joy

- McClure, Vimala. "Peace." *The Tao of Motherhood*, Calif: New World Library, 1997, 20.

### *The Many Levels of I: From the Mundane to the Sublime*

- Sarkar, P.R. "Vibration, Form and Color", *Subhásita Samgraha* Part 3, Electronic Edition 9: the Works of P.R. Sarkar, 2018.

### *The Bond of Silence: Listening from Within*

- Bussey, Marcus. *Gurukul Webinar "Evolution of Consciousness: A Neohumanist Story."* Feb. 22, 2014. http://gurukul.edu/resourcesx/webinars-archive/
- Sarkar, P.R. "Vibration, Form and Color." *Subhásita Samgraha Part 3*, Electronic Edition 9: the Works of P.R. Sarkar, 2018.

### *The Hearts and Minds of Meditating Mothers*

- Napthali, Sarah. *Buddhism for Mothers*. Australia: Inspired Living, NSW, 2003, 11.
- Sarkar, P.R. "Indukamala to Lyatta.", *Shabdha Cayanika 2*, Electronic Edition 9: the Works of P.R. Sarkar, 2018.
- Milojevic, Ivana, *personal correspondence with author*.
- Sarkar, P.R. "The Supreme Question." *Subhásita Samgraha 6*, Electronic Edition 9: the Works of P.R. Sarkar, 2018.

### Meditation and Mantras: Focusing on the Goal, Not the Obstacles

- Sarkar, P.R. "The Macrocosmic Stance and Human Life." *Subhásita Samgraha, Part 7,* Electronic Edition 9: the Works of P.R. Sarkar, 2018.
- Hanson, Rick. "Neuroscience of Happiness." *Greater Good Podcast,* Greater Good Science Center, University of California, Berkely, 9/22/10; "Confronting the Negativity Bias." https://www.rickhanson.net
- Maria Montessori, http://www.dailymontessori.com/maria-montessori-quotes/

### Recapturing Mysticism: The Soul of Meditation

- Ahmed, Akbar. *Rumi Returning: The Triumph of Divine Passion.* Documentary directed by Kell Kearns, 2007.
- Sarkar, P.R. "Mysticism and Spirituality." *Ananda Vacanamrtam 23,* Electronic Edition 9: the Works of P.R. Sarkar, 2018.
- Jalal al-Din Rumi Documentary, *Rumi Returning: The Triumph of Divine Passion.* Directed by Kell Kearns, 2007.
- Sarkar, P.R. "Vrajagopala and Bhaktitattva." *Namami Krsna Sundaram.* Electronic Edition 9: the Works of P.R. Sarkar, 2018.
- Sarkar, P.R. "Vidya Tantra and Avidya Tantra." *Discourses on Tantra Vol 2.* Electronic Edition 9: the Works of P.R. Sarkar, 2018.

## Ch 5 Pregnant Love

### The Good, the Hard, and All That's In-between

- Alban Gosline, Andrea & Lisa Burnett, *Celebrating Motherhood,* Berkely, Calif: Conari Press, 1999, 2002, 74.
- Lerner, Harriet. *The Mother Dance: How Children Change Your Life.* New York: Harper Collins, 1999, part 1, Initiation.
- Stadlen, Naomi. *How Mothers Love and How Relationships Are Born.* London: Piatkus Publishing, 2011, 13.

### Coordinated Cooperation: Partners from the Beginning

- Lokugamage, Amali. *The Heart in the Womb: An Exploration into the Roots of Human Love and Social Cohesion.* Docamali Ltd., 2011, 13.
- Svoboda, Robert. *Ayurveda: Life, Health and Longevity.* Albuquerque: Ayurvedic Press, 2004, 107.

### The Two-in-One Phenomenon

- Zohar, Danah. *The Quantum Self.* London: Bloomsbury Publishing, 1990, 108.
- Steingraber, Sandra. *Having Faith: An Ecologist's Journey to Motherhood.* Cambridge, Mass: Perseus Publishing, 2001.
- Svoboda, Robert. *Ayurveda: Life, Health and Longevity.* Albuquerque: Ayurvedic Press, 2004, 107.

- Schwartz, Eugene. Waldorf Education lecture series: "New Paradigms in Parenting." http://www.millennialchild.com/Resources/podcasts.html

**Asking the Big Questions**
- Sarkar, P.R. "The Three Factors for Spiritual Elevation."; "The Three Prerequisites for Spiritual Knowledge."; "The Three Vital Factors." *Ananda Vacanamrtam 1, 4, 33,* Electronic Edition 9: the Works of P.R. Sarkar, 2018.
- Brizendine, Louann. *The Female Brain.* New York: Broadway Books, 2006), 98-100.
- The Commission for Children at Risk. "Hardwired to Connect: The New Scientific Case for Authoritative Communities" sponsored by the Institute for American Values, YMCA of the USA, and Dartmouth Medical School; *Shift: At the Frontiers of Consciousness,* publication of the Institute of Noetic Sciences, No 8, September-November 2005, 14.
- Zohar, Danah and Ian Marshall. *Spiritual Intelligence, the Ultimate Intelligence,* London: Bloomsbury Publishing Plc., 2000, 202.

## Ch 6 Birth Love

### Being Born and Giving Birth: Tantric Struggle and Surrender
- Alban Gosline, Andrea and Lisa Burnett. *Celebrating Motherhood,* Calif: Conari Press, 1990, 2002, 135.
- Newman, Robert Bruce. Michel Odent quote, from Birth Reborn, 1994; *Calm Birth: New Method for Conscious Childbirth.* Calif: North Atlantic Books, 2005, 164.
- Lerner, Harriet. *Mother Dance: How Children Change Your Life.* Harper Collins E-book, 1999, Part 1 - Initiation.
- Sarkar, P.R. "Sadhana." *Discourses on Tantra, Vol 2,* Calcutta: Ananda Marga Publications, 1994, 10.
- Leboyer, Frederick. New Earth Records interview, August 2006, www.newearthrecords.com/music-store/videos/
- Sarkar, P.R. "Vibration, Form and Color." *Subhásita Samgraha* Part 3, Electronic Edition 9: the Works of P.R. Sarkar, 2018.

### The Birthing Mind: Maintaining Inner Focus
- Documentary on Jalal al-Din Rumi, *Rumi Returning: The Triumph of Divine Passion.* Directed by Kell Kearns, 2007.
- Sarkar, P.R. "Saincara and Pranah" *Ananda Marga Philosophy in a Nutshell 1,* Electronic Edition 9: the Works of P.R. Sarkar, 2018.

### The Birthing Mind: Maintaining Outer Balance
- Documentary on Jalal al-Din Rumi, *Rumi Returning: The Triumph of Divine Passion.* Directed by Kell Kearns, 2007,

- Luce et al. "Is it Realistic?' The Portrayal of Pregnancy and Childbirth in the Media." *BMC Pregnancy and Childbirth,* 2016, 16:40 DOI 10.1186/ s12884-016-0827-x.

**Birth Attendants**
- Wagner, Marsden. "Choosing Caesarean Section." *Midwifery Today,* Issue 57, Spring 2001. http://www.midwiferytoday.com/articles/ choosingcaesarean.asp
- Fahy, Kathleen, Maralyn Foureur, and Carolyn Hastie. *Birth Territory and Midwifery Guardianship: Theory for Practice, Education and Research,* quoting Michele Odent Penna: Elsevier Ltd., 2008, 147.

**The Place of Birth**
- Chilton Pearce, Joseph. "Pregnancy, Birth and Bonding." from the video series *Reaching Beyond the Magical Child,* 1984, Touch the Future https:// ttfuture.org.

**Difficult Births: Trauma, Time and Healing**
- Svanberg, Dr. Emma. *Make Birth Better.* https://www.makebirthbetter.org/ what-is-birth-trauma
- Kitzinger, Sheila. "When a Bad Birth Haunts You." *Prima Baby, Oct/Nov 2000.*
- Wright, Jody. article in *Parenting from the Heart,* Mass: Motherwear Inc., 1996, 83.
- Jameson Griebenow, Jennifer. "Healing the Trauma: Entering Motherhood with Post Traumatic Stress Disorder (PTSD)." *Midwifery Today,* Int. Midwife, 2006, Winter; (80):28-31, 68.
- Lynn Madsen quoted by Jameson Griebenow, Jennifer. ibid.

**Samskara and Birth: All Part of a Bigger Plan**
- Sarkar, P.R. "Science of Action." *Ananda Marga Karma Sannyasa in a Nutshell,* Electronic Edition 9: the Works of P.R. Sarkar, 2018.
- Sarkar, P.R. "What is My Relation to the Universe and the Cosmic Entity?" *Ananda Marga Elementary Philosophy,* Electronic Edition 9: the Works of P.R. Sarkar, 2018.

**Ch 7 After-birth Love**

**Who is This New Me?**
- Hall, Jennifer. Reva Rubin excerpted from *Midwifery, Mind and Spirit* Oxford: Elsevier Ltd., 2001), 64.
- Bergum, Vangie. *Woman to Mother: A Transformation.* Mass: Bergin and Garvey, 1989.
- Kabat-Zinn, Jon. interview with KidscareCanada, www.kidscarecanada.org

- Sarkar, P.R. "Don't Be Misguided" *Ananda Vacanamrtam 5,,* Electronic Edition 9: the Works of P.R. Sarkar, 2018.

### A Mother's Unique Self
- McClure, Vimala. *The Path of Parenting,* Novato, Calif: New World Library, 1999, 2.
- Stern, Daniel and Nadia Bruschweiler Stern. *The Birth of a Mother.* New York: Basic Books, 1998, 13.
- Griscom, Rufus & Alisa Volkman. *Let's Talk Parenting Taboos.* TED talk, TEDWomen, Dec. 2010, http://www.ted.com/talks/rufus_griscom_alisa_volkman_let_s_talk_parenting_taboos
- Morgan Elisa and Carol Kuykendall. *Real Moms: Exploding the Myths of Motherhood.* Grand Rapids, Michigan: Zondervan, 2002, 24.
- Morrison, Toni. *Conversations with Toni Morrison* Jackson, Miss.: University Press of Mississippi, 1994, 270-271.

### Bountiful Mother's Milk
- Davidson, Richard J. and Anne Harrington. *Dalai Lama: Visions of Compassion.* New York: Oxford University Press, 2002, 70-71.
- Simms, Eva. *The Child in the World: Embodiment, Time and Language in Early Childhood.* Michigan: Wayne State University Press, 2008, 11-12.
- Dick-Read, Dr. Grantly. *Childbirth Without Fear.* http://www.llli.org

### Expect the Unexpected: The Only Constant in Life Is Change
- Sarkar, P.R. "Sadvipra, Taraka Brahma, Sadashiva and Shrii Krsna." Ananda Vacanamrtam 8, Electronic Edition 9: the Works of P.R. Sarkar, 2018.
- Stadlen, Naomi. *What Mothers Do Especially When It Looks Like Nothing.* New York: Penguin Books, 2004, 14.
- Zohar, Danah and Ian Marshall. *Spiritual Intelligence, the Ultimate Intelligence.* London: Bloomsbury Publishing Plc., 2000, p13.

### Intuition Travels on Love: Heart Communication
- Chilton Pearce, Joseph. "Pregnancy, Birth and Bonding." from the video series *Reaching Beyond the Magical Child,* 1984, Touch the Future, https://ttfuture.org
- Franquemont, Sharon. "Intuition Travels on Love." interview on *Sounds True* podcast, July 30, 2013, and www.intuitionworks.com
- Institute of HeartMath. "Heart Intelligence." August 7, 2012, *htps://www.heartmath.org*
- Armour, J. Andrew. "The Little Brain on the Heart." https://www.ccjm.org/content/ccjom/74/2_suppl_1/S48.full.pdf
- Alebrahim, Khaled. "The Intellectual Heart." January 2016, *https://www.researchgate.net/publication/307410420_The_intellectual_heart*

- Sarkar, P.R. "Mind, Pranendriya and Vritti." *Idea and Ideology.* Electronic Edition 9: the Works of P.R. Sarkar, 2018.
- Sarkar, P.R. "The Ascent of Mind." *Subhásita Samgraha* 8, Electronic Edition 9: the Works of P.R. Sarkar, 2018.

### Beyond Human Love: What Next?
- King, Ursula. Spirit of Fire: The Life and Vision of Teilhard de Chardin. New York: Orbis Books, 2015, 113.
- Sarkar, P.R. Ananda Sutram. Calcutta: Ananda Marga Publications, 1967, 19.

## Ch 8 Children Raising Parents

### Mothermaking
- Prasa, Rama and Caroline Robertson. Peter Devries quote in *Divine Delivery*, Ayurveda Elements, http://ayurvedaelements.com/articledivinedelivery.php

### Children as Teachers
- McClure, Vimala. *The Path of Parenting*. Novato, Calif.: New World Library, 1999, 4.
- Chilton Pearce, Joseph. Introduction to Tobin Hart's *The Secret Spiritual Life of Children*. Hawaii: Inner Ocean Publishing, 2003, x.

### Dharmic Qualities Children Can Teach Us
- Kabat-Zinn, Jon. Interview with KidscareCanada, www.kidscarecanada.org
- Sarkar, P.R. "Safeguards against the Defects of Jinana and Karma." *Ananda Vacanamrtam 23,* Electronic Edition 9: the Works of P.R. Sarkar, 2018.

### SQ: Children's Natural Spiritual Intelligence
- Armstrong, Thomas. T*he Radiant Child*. London: The Theosophical Publishing House, 1988, 2.
- Zohar, Danah and Ian Marshall. *Spiritual Intelligence, the Ultimate Intelligence.* London: Bloomsbury Publishing Plc. 2000, 193-194.

## Ch 9 The Yogic Mind

### From Bliss to Body and Back Again
- Sarkar, P.R. "This World and the Next." *Subhásita Samgraha part 4,* Electronic Edition 9: the Works of P.R. Sarkar, 2018.
- Zohar, Danah and Ian Marshall. *Spiritual Intelligence, the Ultimate Intelligence.* London: Bloomsbury Publishing Plc., 2000, 152.

### The Physical Body
- Gerhardt, Sue. *Why Love Matters*. New York: Routledge, 2004, 22.

- Huffington, Arianna. "My Conversation with co-sleeping expert James McKenna." *Huffington Post*. April 22, 2015, https://www.huffpost.com/entry/james-mckenna-co-sleeping-expert_b_7119782
- McKenna, James. "Co-sleeping with infants: Science, Public Policy, and Parents Civil Rights." *Mother-Baby Behavioral Sleep Laboratory, Notre Dame University*, https://cosleeping.nd.edu
- Hinde, Katie. "The Complexities of Breast Milk." Arizona State University Center for Evolution and Medicine, https://evmed.asu.edu/news/complexities-breast-milk
- International Association of Infant Massage. "The Benefits of Infant Massage."
- https://iaim.net/benefits/
- MJ Glassman, *personal correspondence with author*
- McKenna et al, "Human Infant Biology and Its Relationship to Parental Caregiving." *Mother-Baby Behavioral Sleep Laboratory, Notre Dame University*, https://cosleeping.nd.edu/assets/46497/western_constraints_on_the_fairest_love.pdf

### *The Root or Conscious Mind*
- Stern, Daniel N. *Diary of a Baby*. New York: Basic Books, 1998, 47-48.

### *The Intellectual, Emotional or Subconscious Mind*
- Sarkar, P.R. "Questions and Answers on Yoga Psychology." *Yoga Psychology*, Electronic Edition 9: the Works of P.R. Sarkar, 2018.
- Stadlen, Naomi. *What Mothers Do Especially When It Looks Like Nothing*. New York: Penguin Books, 2004, 153.

### *The Supramental Unconscious Mind*
- Inayat Khan, Hazrat. "The Education of the Infant." *The Sufi Message of Hazrat Inayat Khan,* Vol. 3, ch 1,

### *The Subliminal Unconscious Mind*
- Porac, Clare. "Holding Babies: Why is the Left Side Favored?" *In Your Hands*, Penn State, May 2016, https://sites.psu.edu/clarep/2016/05/17/holding-babies-why-is-the-left-side-favored/

### *Golden Kosa: the Pure Unconscious Mind*
- de Chardin, Pierre Teillhard. *On Love and Happiness*. New York: Harper &Row, 1984, ch 5.

## Ch 10 Love: The Driving Force of Evolution

### *A Thumbnail Look at Science, Love, Spirituality, and Evolution*
- de Chardin, Pierre Teillhard. *On Love and Happiness*. New York: Harper & Row, 1984.

- Loye, David. Prologue: The Truth About Darwin And Us. http://www. deepleafproductions.com/utopialibrary/text/loye-darwin.html; Comment on Tony Campolo's Critique of Darwinism, Tikkun Magazine, November/December 2010.
- Lipton, Bruce. "What Our Cells Can Teach Us". *Sounds True Podcast Insights on the Edge.*https://www.resources.soundstrue.com/transcript/what-our-cells-can-teach-us/
- Maturana Romesin, Humberto and Gerda Verden-Zoller, *Biology Of Love* Opp, G.: Peterander, F. (Hrsg.): Focus Heilpädagogik, Ernst Reinhardt, Munchen/Basel, 1996, 8.
- Burunat, Enrique. *Love is the Cause of Human Evolution.* Advances in Anthropology, 2014, 4, 99-116.
- Beauregard, Mario and Denyse O'Leary. *Spiritual Brain: A Neuroscientist's Case for the Existence of the Soul.* New York: Harper Collins, 2007, 295.
- Newberg, Andrew. *Why God Won't Go Away.* New York: Random House, 2001, 145-146.
- Vaillant, George. *Spiritual Evolution.* New York: Broadway Books, 2008, 7, 16.

### Tantric Evolution and the Attraction of Infinite Love

- Sarkar, P.R. "Longing for the Great." *Subhásita Samgraha part 24,* Electronic Edition 9: the Works of P.R. Sarkar, 2018.
- Sarkar, P.R. "Evolution Towards Perfection." *Subhásita Samgraha II,* Electronic Edition 9: the Works of P.R. Sarkar, 2018.
- Sarkar, P.R. "Aspects of Devotional Sentiment and Neohumanism." *The Liberation of Intellect: Neohumanism.* Electronic Edition 9: the Works of P.R. Sarkar, 2018.

### Mother-Child Love and Evolution: Where Is It Going?

- Sarkar, P.R. "The True Nature of Bhakti." *Ananda Vacanamrtam 7,* Electronic Edition 9: the Works of P.R. Sarkar, 2018.
- Sarkar, P.R. "Women's Right." *The Awakening of Women.* Electronic Edition 9: the Works of P.R. Sarkar, 2018.

# About Ananda Marga

Ananda Marga is a socio-spiritual movement founded by Shrii Shrii Anandamurti (P.R. Sarkar) in 1955. The goal of life is understood to be spiritual self-realization and the means to that goal is service to self and others. These concepts are embodied in the three pillars of Ananda Marga: Tantra Yoga, the practical, mystical path to realization; Neohumanism, a philosophy designed to elevate humanism to the level of universalism; and the socio-economic principles of the Progressive Utilization Theory (PROUT).

The teaching of Ananda Marga philosophy and practices as well as diverse service projects are integral parts of the many centers around the world. We welcome you to contact us and join us in our journey